How to Becc Successful: Creative Ways to Make Money with a Side Hustle

How to Become a Millionaire - Learn the Best Passive Income Ideas

By Dr. Ernesto Martinez

www.AttaBoyCowboy.com

Also by Ernesto Martinez

How to Become Rich and Successful. The Secret of Success and the Habits of Successful People. Entrepreneurship and Developing Entrepreneur Characteristics

How to Travel the World and Live with No Regrets. Learn How to Travel for Free, Find Cheap Places to Travel, and Discover Life-Changing Travel Destinations.

How to Boost Your Credit Score Range and Make Money with Credit Cards. How to Repair Your Credit with Credit Repair Strategies.

How to Heal Broken Bones Faster. Bone Fracture Healing Tips. Learn About Bone Fracture Healing Foods, Types of Bone Fractures, and the Five Stages of Bone Healing.

How to Lose Weight Without Dieting or Exercise. Over 250 Ways. Learn About Foods that Burn Fat, Weight Loss Diets, Weight Loss Tips, Weight Loss Foods, and How to Lose Belly Fat

ISBN: 978-1-64635-004-9 eBook, 978-1-64635-005-6 Paperback

DEDICATION

To my friend Charles Blunt and the profound impact, he had on my life. I will always cherish our special times together and remember the beautiful things he taught me. Charles was a real man; kind, generous, funny, compassionate, honest, hardworking, and selfless.

All for one and one for all my friend, what fun we had. The times we shared Brothers 'til the end. Love always Ernesto. God Bless!

Preface

O n this stunning new book, Dr. Ernesto Martinez offers us a step-by-step guide on the best and the most successful ideas to start your own business. He asks the question: what can you do now to increase your income?

His answer is that there is a new labor market forming in this global workplace brimming with opportunities for those that are willing to act now and be bold! This basket of opportunities is creating new businesses and industries.

Technology is making it possible to integrate workers from around the world with ease. The changes we are seeing are happening exponentially faster than they have in the past, and people who are not transitioning are missing out on opportunities.

How to Become Rich and Successful: Creative Ways to Make Money with a Side Hustle Subtitle: How to Become a Millionaire - Learn the Best Passive Income Ideas will give you the pathways to starting new businesses to pursue and form the life you've always wanted.

"Dr. Ernesto Martinez offers strategies to start your own businesses immediately! A treasure chest of advice and information that any entrepreneur can follow and implement. I highly recommend this book for anyone interested in starting a new business." John Sendrey Software Engineer, startup incubator, and professional Side Hustler.

Table of Contents

Introduction

G rowing up in Los Angeles, California, has been a dream. One of the benefits of growing up in a big city is that you get the opportunity to be around people from all over the world. The universities I attended all tried to outdo each other by saying theirs was the most diverse university in the world. They claimed to have students from every continent on the planet, and to have dozens of languages being spoken on campus every day. They were right, every class I attended, every job and neighborhood was a mixture of people from different parts of the world. I went to a party this weekend with people from seventeen countries and food from ten. This diversity gives you the opportunity to learn and to be exposed to ideas that would otherwise be difficult to come across. One of the most important things you learn is how to hustle!

Big cities tend to attract people who are hungry for opportunities and who are willing to work hard to get ahead. You're around people who are ambitious, street smart, and who most likely grew up poor in some other part of the world. These people see the USA as a basket of opportunities, and they open your eyes to the gold mine we're all sitting on.

The workplace is now becoming a world worksite interconnected with people from all over the planet and becoming more and more so rapidly. Technology is making it possible to integrate workers from around the world with ease. The changes we are seeing are happening exponentially faster than they have in the past, and people who are not transitioning are missing out on opportunities.

The first major change is the introduction of robots. In 2017, robots could perform 90% of the jobs that humans did. It is only a matter of time for new robots to come online and for humans to transition to a strategic and managerial role. Robots will increase our overall productivity and the quality of life for humans will increase as robots automate many of the job's humans used to do. As the transition to robots accelerates, humans will need to become better trained and educated to coexist with automation.

The second major change is globalization. More of the work you do is broken up into pieces that are performed in different parts of the planet. This creates opportunities for those who are flexible and learn to increase their productivity by leveraging other people's expertise to help them do their job better.

The third major shift is people working at home via telecommuting instead of going to the office. Forty-three percent of Americans now work from home on varying schedules. This is causing a more relaxed and less formal work environment.

The fourth major shift is towards temporary and part-time work, also known as a 'side hustle'. This term got its start in the 1950s when it was used to describe both legitimate jobs and scams. A side hustle is any job taken in addition to your full-time job. A side hustle is usually freelance or part-time and is meant to provide supplemental income. Side hustles are earning an average of $686 a month in 2019. Thirty-seven percent of Americans and fifty-nine percent of millennials have side hustles.

Being aware of these changes will help you stay ahead of what's coming and make adjustments so you're able to take advantage of the opportunities that will be available. Keys to success; stay up to date with changes and find your place in these new situations. Be flexible to changes and responsibilities. Do not avoid changes; be willing to change with the times. Do not be intimidated by the pace or type of changes, instead try to take advantage of them. Keep learning and acquiring new skills that would increase your value and give you more value in the marketplace. As long as you continue to adjust as changes come along, you'll make yourself an asset and your earning potential will increase.

Chapter 1 Rent out Space in Your Driveway

I used to have two cars, even though I could only drive one at a time. I decided to sell the extra car, invest the money from the sale, and start renting out the additional parking spaces in my driveway. I have five parking spaces in my driveway. I rented four parking spaces for $175 each per month for a total of $700 a month and $8400 a year. Some of the cars are never even moved as the owners have collector cars that they want to store. I have not had any inconvenience at all, and the cars make it seem like someone is always at home which has been an added safety feature. There are websites, such as Parking Cupid, CurbFlip, Pavemint, or ParkEasier, that allow you to list your parking spaces for long term or day use.

Chapter 2 Renting Your Place Short Term

I live in a studio house and rent it out two days a week for $200 a night. I take my mom and dad out for a lovely evening and spend the night. Or I pay for my weekend getaway somewhere by renting my house for the weekend. On weekends hotels are the most expensive, so it's easy to rent, and you can get a higher return per night. It generates an extra $1,600 a month or $19,200 a year for me. When I decided to update my kitchen, I just rented out my house for more time, and I got my new kitchen for free. When I want to stay at home, I don't accept reservations. Flip Key, Airbnb, Furnished Finder, Transplant Housing, HomeAway are good sites to get started on for short term rentals. Make sure you check the laws in your city, so you don't get burned.

Chapter 3 Real Estate Acquisition

In my opinion, real estate acquisition is the number one way to get rich, or super rich, on a very consistent basis. When it comes to technology or stocks, you can make it big, but the risks are much greater. Most millionaires are still made in real estate. Around the year two thousand, I read that over ninety percent of millionaires in California were made in real estate. Since then, that has changed due to the surge in technology companies. But at the time, this gave me something to focus on and start learning. Within four years, I had great success. Real estate has many benefits because people are always going to need housing; and with the current exponential and unchecked growth of the human population, there will surely be someone needing a place to live if you have a place for rent.

Real estate is a hedge against inflation. If inflation starts increasing, your rents and property values will increase with inflation. As the cost of living goes up, so will your cash flow. Your properties will give you tax benefits, passive income, property value appreciation, and leverage. Leverage is the most important factor because it allows you to make a lot of money fast off someone else's money. Leveraging, of course, only works if your borrowed investment increases in value more than the money you borrowed. This is how leveraging works; let us say, you have twenty thousand dollars, you invest it in an investment account, and at the end of the year you earn ten percent interest, and your gains would be two thousand dollars. However, if you invest that twenty thousand into buying a two hundred-thousand-dollar house and finance the other one hundred eighty thousand dollars and that house appreciates by ten percent, then your gains would be twenty thousand dollars, and because your initial investment was twenty thousand and you made twenty thousand, then your return on investment was one hundred percent instead of ten percent in the first scenario. This isn't taking into account the rents, depreciation, nor the tax benefits you can get from the property.

Chapter 4 Make use of Empty Space

Peerspace is a peer-to-peer marketplace for renting out unused space by the hour at specific times for events, meetings, and productions. Peerspace charges 15% of the total booking amount to hosts, there are no membership fees, and it's free to list. Businesses can rent out their location or office after hours for various professional and social purposes such as offices, culinary activities, fitness, studios, events, production, performances, and classes. Users can rent spaces for their events and pay by the hour, and hosts can help recoup some of the costs they pay for rent.

Chapter 5 Flip Real Estate

Research properties in your area through websites like TheMLS, Zillow, HomeFinder, or ZipRealty, and find a property that is below market value, usually, because the property is being foreclosed, owners need a quick sale, or the property is in bad condition. When you find one negotiate the price ($220,000 purchase price), figure out how much it would cost you to fix the property ($40,000 repairs), and add that to your estimated purchase price for a total ($260,000). Figure out what that house would sell for if you bought it and fixed it up ($300,000 sale price) and see if the profit ($40,000) is worth your effort. This is something that depends on your earning potential, and how long you estimate it'll take you to fix the property and sell it. If making $40,000 in three months is a good deal for you, and it's more than you would make doing something else, then it's a good investment. But, if your contractor says it'll take six months to fix the place (instead of a month) and the houses in the area are on the market for about six months before they sell according to realty websites, then you have to figure out if it's worth it to make $40,000 over the course of a year. The good thing about this type of deal is that it can be a side job and you can still have other businesses going on while you remodel the house. Flipping houses is ideal for people who know something about construction and would like to start working for themselves fixing the houses they are buying and reselling them.

You also must figure in other costs such as holding costs for the loans to buy the property, interest on repair loans, fees for the real estate agent to sell it, and any other costs you may incur. Generally, this is a pretty straight forward business, and the better you are at doing repairs with your own crew, the more you're going to save, and the more you're going to make. You will also learn other strategies to save on expenses like selling your own house for sale by owner (FSBO) sites or Craigslist, buying directly from the owners to save on commissions, making owner financed sales to save on bank fees, and using your low-interest credit card balance transfer offers to make the repairs or even to purchase the properties.

Here is a strategy for becoming rich and even super rich. Use the real estate acquisition strategy with leveraging to keep buying and buying more properties to rent or flip them.

One of my colleagues bought over forty buildings here in Los Angeles by leveraging them one by one and buying more. Generally, you start this with regular investment loans, and as you scale up, you use private money loans. He would buy one for $300,000 with $30,000 down. Fix it up, start renting it, and once the property value went up some, he would take a line of credit or refinance the house and use that money to acquire another property, and just keep repeating the process over and over.

The first way to increase the property value is to raise the rents, because you increase the cash flow on the real estate. The second way is property appreciation which can happen by either you are making upgrades and remodeling or simply the general market increasing in price. If you can keep finding ways to increase your property value, you can keep leveraging your properties pulling money out of them and buying more. If the property prices stop appreciating, which is cyclical and happens around every seven years, you simply hold on and just keep renting your properties till the next price upswing, and then continue the same strategy.

What if there is a large price drop in the property prices? In 2008, I had one property drop from being valued at $500,000 to $160,000 in about one year; this happened to me several times. The interesting thing was that rents increased during this time as people got scared and allowed the banks to foreclose on their homes and they were pushed into the rental market. So, I ended up making more money than ever during the real estate downturn, because I stuck to my investment plan of buying, fixing, and renting.

Just do not get scared, the market will eventually recover as people keep reproducing and they need a place to live. In this example, that property went back up to $750,000 about eight years later. Meanwhile, I kept making money from the rents, because I focused on the cash flow and not on the property value. As long as I was paying $1,200 a month for mortgage and expenses and I was taking in $2,000 in rent, making $800 in profit or $9,600 a year, what difference did it make what the property was worth? Sure, I was concerned watching my net worth and the property values declining, but I knew it was temporary and I kept making money on the property. So don't get rattled and give up, or you'll be stuck on the sidelines for about seven years till your credit recovers. Had I allowed the banks to foreclose on my properties so I did not have to absorb the temporary property value drops, I would have lost the opportunity to cash in when the properties were recovering, and I would have lost all of the rental income, which went from $2,000 a month to over $6,000 a month eight years later and the mortgage stayed the same $1,200. So I was making $4,800 a month or $57,600 a year on that same property.

Another way to look at properties is not to consider them yours. This helps break the material attachment to them when you have to make decisions to sell or demolish them. They actually belong to the banks, because they own the note on the property and you're just a tenant of theirs. The bank is your partner, and your job is to make the property as productive as possible so you don't default and you can earn something for your work.

Chapter 6 Real Estate Wholesaler

Real estate wholesalers search for distressed properties (people behind on payments), fixer-uppers, and properties for sale that are below market price so they can connect buyers with sellers. When you find properties at a reasonable price compared to other properties in the area, you contact the seller, obtain the sales contract, negotiate the price, and present the property to buyers. You earn the difference between your negotiated contract price and the eventual sales price. You will earn revenue through a wholesaling fee attached to the transaction, typically a percentage of the property cost. Buyers are usually real estate investors who prefer not to spend time searching for discounted properties or negotiating with sellers.

Since it does not require you to have any capital, wholesaling is an excellent way to start investing in real estate. Wholesaling is a perfect way to learn about the real estate market and master negotiation skills.

Chapter 7 Become a Home Inspector

When buying a house, the buyer hires a home inspector to examine a home and identify any significant issues before closing. Any problems discovered can be used as points of negotiation with the seller. A home inspector has to get certified, get liability insurance, and follow local regulations. Home inspections can cost $400 and up.

Chapter 8 Deputy Inspector

When someone builds something, the city has to come out and inspect the work as you complete milestones to make sure the job is up to code. However, the city does not want the building and safety inspector to verify all of the work themselves, or the city would assume all of the risks if something were to go wrong. Therefore, the city spreads the risk by certifying third-party deputy inspectors to check the work. Becoming a deputy inspector requires taking some certification classes then being tested by the city. A deputy inspector usually comes out for about five minutes, writes a report, and bills approximately $250-350 for a visit before heading to the next stop.

Chapter 9 Construction Project Manager

Construction project managers oversee the planning and completion of construction projects. They ensure that the project is on time, pull permits as needed, coordinate with different trades, meet with inspectors, budget, and communicate with stakeholders. Their job is to make sure everything flows, problem-solve, and ensure the job is on schedule. Volunteering or an apprenticeship is essential to learn how the process works. However, once you know what is required to complete projects, you can check in on an as-needed basis.

Chapter 10 Property Manager

In many areas, once you have more than a certain number of units, you're required to have a property manager on site. A property manager (sometimes called a real estate manager) is a person or firm charged with the day-to-day management of real estate property in exchange for a monetary fee or free or reduced rent. When the owner cannot personally attend to such details or is not interested in doing so. The schedule can range from taking calls from tenants and addressing whatever needs come up to living onsight with daily office hours. The property manager's responsibilities may include:

Supervising and coordinating building maintenance and work orders.

Doing light handyman and cleaning work.

Resolving tenant concerns and complaints.

Advertising.

Showing and leasing vacant units.

Collecting and depositing rent.

Communicating regularly with the owners or tenants.

Chapter 11 Home Stager

One of our past tenants used to add decor, rearrange furniture, dress up her home to look stunning, take photos for her blog site, and eventually used them in a book she wrote called "The New Bohemians'. Ultimately, she became a world-renown designer and making a great living from staging her home.

Home staging is a marketing tactic that can make even the darkest, drab space feel bright, energetic, and homey. Staging aims to make a home appealing to the highest number of potential buyers, thereby selling or renting a property more swiftly and for more money. Build a relationship with landlords, real estate agents, and investors for repeat business staging their properties.

Chapter 12 Renting Furniture for Home Staging

A successful stager will have to use the right furniture for the demographic. Most stagers will use furniture from furniture rental companies. However, if you are trying to appeal to a specific demographic, rental companies may not have the details you need to dress up your property. For example, in our Los Angeles neighborhood, the bohemian style is what most attracts renters and buyers. And this type of decor includes used and antique furniture that is not as easy to find. So, we've built up a stash of items that we rent out or use in our staging projects to help properties move faster. Make a website with pictures of your staged properties with your items, descriptions, prices, and send the information to stagers in your community.

Chapter 13 Real Estate Crowdfunding

You can buy individual shares of real estate property through websites like RealtyMogul, Fundrise, Groundbreaker, CrowdStreet, Groundfloor, RealCrowd, RealtyShares, or Patch of Land. According to these sites, investors can earn an average of twelve to fifteen percent annually on their investment. This helps reduce the risk you may incur by investing in real estate ventures on your own. It also allows you to invest in real estate, even when you don't have much money to start investing.

Chapter 14 Make Money by Peer-to-Peer Lending

Prosper, LendingClub, Peerform, Upstart, and Kiva are some of the peer-to-peer lending websites you can use to lend your own money to others with return depending on how much risk you're willing to accept. People who have lower credit scores are charged more interest since they are considered higher risk. So, you make more on those investments. While people who have higher credit scores represent a lower risk of default. So, investing in their loans pays less interest. I've tried both categories. The people who had lower credit scores tended to default more often, which wiped out my earnings. You can also diversify and spread your risk across several people in small loans as small as a few dollars. This helps to lower your risk even further.

Chapter 15 Round Up Your Purchases with Acorns

Acorns automatically invests your spare change into a portfolio of ETFs. Every time you swipe your card, you can round it up to the nearest dollar and have it funded. You have the option for Roundups, recurring investments, or one-time investments as little as five dollars. As the market fluctuates, your investments are automatically rebalanced across more than 7,000 stocks and bonds. This is a way to make sure you are saving and investing something for your future throughout the year.

Chapter 16 Consider Your Credit Cards as Investment Tools

Remember that many credit card interest payments can exceed even mortgage payments. So be careful! This technique is called stoozing or credit card arbitrage. Rather than using your credit cards to rack up high-interest debt that's the worst kind you can accumulate. Develop a disciplined approach to using your credit cards as investment tools. Use credit card offers to leverage low-interest loans to use on non-risky investments. There is a range of credit card offers available hoping you'll rack up bad debt buying consumer goods then get stuck paying over 20% for the life of the loan. This is often the start of people's financial problems, getting stuck with high-interest consumer debt.

However, you can use these credit card offers to your

advantage by taking advantage of the balance transfer offers at zero interest for eighteen months and a 3% processing fee. Balance transfers mean you can transfer other consumer debt onto your card, or you can move the funds into your bank account. With these terms, it works out to a 2% loan per year over the eighteen months, which is below inflation and gives you the ability to leverage or invest the credit card company's money to work for you.

Inflation in the USA averages 3% per year, so a loan at 2% per year would mean you're making 1% per year on the loan. Managing these transactions takes discipline, or you could end up in the worst position.

Some of the investments I consider making are in fixed interest or dividend paying funds. Such as Clean Capital or Wunder Capital's solar funds that offer a 7 1/2% return on investment and the credit card charging 2%, you end up making 5.5% on the loan. Although the investment is for five years, it makes monthly payments into your bank account, and you have eighteen months to pay back the money you borrowed. So make sure you don't borrow more than you can pay back in eighteen months with your extra income, or expected income, over the eighteen month period. Meanwhile, you invested in the fund that is generating revenue for you, and it's going to keep doing so for five years.

Another way to look at it is basically borrowing the money from your credit card to invest before you actually have the money. But you're expecting to be able to save the amount you borrowed over the eighteen-month period and pay it back. So you get to invest the credit card money for eighteen months for only 3%, and because you're expecting to make 7.5%, it's a sweet deal.

The other benefit is that it forces you to save your money and have eighteen months of earnings before you actually have the money.

Another option is Worthy Capital which pays 5% and allows you to put money in and take it out whenever you want, so you can make 3% for the term of the credit card loan, pay back the money, and keep the interest you made. Every eighteen months after you've paid off the balance on your credit card, you can keep repeating the same sequence borrowing the money again, investing it, and building up another investment for eighteen months. If you have a card with a $50,000 spending limit, you can make $1,500 per year on the spread between the interest charged by the credit card and Worthy Capital. If you're using Wunder Capital, you'd make $2,750 per year on the same card before you have to pay it back again. This allows you to leverage the credit card's money, to make money for you.

Chapter 17 Debt Collector

Bill collection is one of the easiest home businesses to start with high profitability and low start-up costs. Because consumer debt is at an all-time high, there are many opportunities for bill and account collectors to attempt to recover payment on overdue bills. They negotiate repayment plans with debtors and help them find solutions to make paying their unpaid bills easier.

You'll need to have good investigative skills to locate a new phone number or address to begin the collections process. If you're empathetic with the debtor, you'll have better results with the collection process than by being condescending and belligerent. It's important to remember that most people who find themselves in debt are going through a difficult time. Being professional and likable is more likely to result in satisfied clients. Most bill collectors get paid once they collect on an account. Rates vary, but they typically keep 20 to 50 percent of the money they collect.

Chapter 18 Repo Man

Also known as a repossession agent, are hired by

banks, debt collection agencies, and other financial institutions to take back possessions from people in debt. To become a repo man, you must learn your state or region's licensing laws and regulations regarding repossession. Then educate yourself on repossession practices and skills. The repo man finds and retrieves vehicles when the owner stops making payments to the lenders. A repo men/woman is compensation for every repossession and the value of the item repossessed. A repossession will bring in between $150 and $450 per car.

Chapter 19 Investing in Startup Companies

This is risky, but not as risky as stock can be, and the returns can be amazing. I recommend using a dollar cost averaging strategy like you would use when buying stock. Just keep investing over a period of time into various startup companies, so that you spread your risk and increase your chances of buying a Unicorn. When you invest in startup companies, you can expect to recover your money in one out of ten investments, and one out of one hundred you can strike it rich with a Unicorn. A Unicorn company is a FaceBook, Google, Uber, Airbnb etc, a company that becomes super successful and you can turn a ten-thousand-dollar investment into a ten-million-dollar investment or better. You have an option of doing the research yourself and investing through websites or picking websites that screen the companies for you. Obviously, the more you do on your own, the greater the share of the profits. Websites such as Wefunder, SeedInvest, StartEngine, AngelList, CircleUp, MicroVentures, EquityZen, and FundersClub allow you to browse companies to make investments in a variety of ranges and options.

Chapter 20 Credit Card Piggybacking

You get paid by credit repair companies to add authorized users (AU) to your credit cards to help them boost their credit scores for loans or other credit inquiries. The AU never knows who you are, and they don't have access to your credit. They are paying for the service of adding your good payment history to their credit report so they can boost their credit report in as little as two weeks. This helps them save long term on interest payments, qualify for loans, and you get paid for adding them onto your account. Your credit company will basically cut and paste your entire card history on to the AU's credit history, which boosts their credit score and saves them money by qualifying them for lower interest rates. Even after you remove them from your account as an AU, your good credit history stays on their account for seven years. There's no potential downside for you because you don't take on their bad credit and they never have access to your accounts to make purchases. I've gotten paid up to $610 for adding someone to my credit card as an AU.

Banks don't allow you to monetize adding authorized users to your accounts, so if you do it too frequently or if you tell them about it, they will close your account. So be responsible.

Chapter 21 Switch to a High-Interest Bank Account

CIT Bank offers a rate of 1.85% on their money market accounts, more than fifteen times the national average. Discover Bank's online savings account offers 1.75%, much higher than the national average. Aspiration offers 2.00% on its savings rate. Aspiration donates 10% of their earnings to the environment, education, water, poverty, human rights, and opportunities for struggling Americans. Varo Money is another option that provides 2.8% on your savings. That's forty-seven times the national average. They all offer free ATM fees and are FDIC-insured.

Chapter 22 Open a Bank Account with Chime

This bank app will allow you to get paid up to two days before your direct deposit posts in your account. They also offer no overdraft fees, no foreign transaction fees, no monthly minimum balance, no ATM fees, and they allow you to round up like Acorns and save money every time you use your card.

Chapter 23 Dividend Investing

Traditional stocks do not provide regular payments to shareholders. The stockholder realizes a profit when the stock increases in share price, and they sell the share for more than they paid for it. Dividend stocks can also be bought and sold, but they also pay out regular dividends. In most cases, stock dividends are paid four times per year or quarterly. Dividend stocks are usually well-established companies such as Coca-Cola or McDonald's with a track record of distributing earnings to shareholders. These types of stocks pay every shareholder a percentage of their profits for every share of stock owned.

Dividend investing is a reliable way for an investor to grow a regular dividend income into lifelong investments and a retirement paycheck. Build your portfolio over time so you create a reliable stream of income.

Set up a free brokerage account at Vanguard, Fidelity, M1 Finance, or any other website that offers long-term investments. Most brokerages provide some free investment counseling for new investors. Robinhood or Betterment is for new investors that want to learn how to trade individual stocks, options, ETFs, or cryptocurrency.

Chapter 24 Women Can Invest in Ellevest

An investment website set up to cater to women's needs. It's a robo-adviser that does gender-based investing in companies that help promote the advancement of women. It also considers female-specific factors such as longer expected life spans than men and lower incomes than men. They do take men as clients, but they are focused on the needs of female clients.

Chapter 25 Join Rize

Rize offers joint checking, savings, and investing, all in one. They automate your savings; you just set your goals, and the app does micro-investing into exchange-traded funds (ETF) to help you reach your short and longer-term financial goals.

Chapter 26 Invest with Robo Investors

EarthFolio allows you to invest in high growth industries solving global challenges. Other apps, like Betterment, Robinhood, Stash, or M1 Finance, charge you fewer fees and give you a variety of flexible options to help you invest. Several of these companies have a sign on bonus for new accounts. Personal Capital or Blooom will analyze your portfolio and provide you with advice on how you could improve your allocation to help you achieve your goals. Investing with apps is the new preferred way for people to invest because of all the free service options that come with it.

Chapter 27 Stay on Top of Your Credit, So It Doesn't Cost You

Credit issues can cost you in lost opportunities and increased borrowing rates. You can monitor your credit with services such as Credit Karma, Credit Sesame, or Credit Works by Experian. These services follow your credit history and inform you when something unusual comes up, or if anything that will affect your credit shows up on your credit; allowing you to try to fix it and get it removed from your credit history before it costs you financially.

Get used to checking your credit history regularly so you can fix mistakes and errors as they appear on your account. One day I had three random phone calls from a low rider custom auto shop, a pizza parlor, and a stereo shop asking me to pay them money for bounced checks. The only problem was that I had never been to the establishments which were all close to where I lived. When I checked my bank account online, I almost cried when I saw that most of the money, I had in my account was gone. I contacted the bank, and they quickly closed my accounts; and after I walked in and signed some documents, they gave me back all the money that was stolen from me. Then the FBI got involved. I didn't find out the details until after the investigation was over. Apparently, some of my mail was stolen from my house; I had some checks in the envelopes and personal information. Enough information for the thieves to start making credit cards, making fake identifications with my information on them, and applying for credit cards in my name. They then went on a shopping spree which led the FBI to get involved. What the FBI found was a house being occupied by about twenty gang members who had a setup to manufacture identification cards and credit cards using people's personal information that they had stolen. It took a few months to get everything off my credit and get my finances back in order. Had I been checking my credit report regularly, I could have stopped some of the damage of the identity theft from happening sooner and avoided some of the mischief that cost me months to fix.

Chapter 28 Micro Investing with Worthy Capital

With as little as ten dollars you can invest your money into Worthy Capital's five percent fixed bonds which is eighty-three times more than you could get from a bank, and you're allowed to pull your money out whenever you want without fees. This is one of my favorite ways to invest money that is sitting in my bank account and that I can't invest long term in something because I may need it.

Chapter 29 Make Money by Saving Money

If you need extra money to pay off high-interest debt, you can apply for a personal loan. Prosper offers low-interest loans with no prepayment penalty. SoFi also provides loans that start at 6.57% with no fees and no prepayment penalty. PersonalLoans.com gives loans up to $35,000 for a variety of lengths of time.

Chapter 30 Become a Freelance Writer

There is always someone out there who wants to read what you think, and you can make a living sharing your ideas with others. There are many options like blogging, ghostwriting, grant writing, or writing content for other websites. If this doesn't appeal to you, then try working as a freelance proofreader, helping other people's creative work sparkle. Some of the options for finding writing work are Grammarly, Contena, Medium, Mediabistro, Paid to Blog, JournalismJobs.com, All Freelance Writing, Freedom With Writing, FWJ (Freelance Writing Jobs), BloggingPro, PubLoft, and Contently. The flexibility is great and you can write from anywhere on the planet.

Chapter 31 Write a Book

Eighty percent of people dream about writing a book. If you decide you want to fulfill this dream, don't be discouraged by seeing multiple titles on the topic you'd like to write about. Most people read many books on the same topic in order to get a better grasp of it.

Now that you can self-publish on Amazon, the barriers to publishing a book are much less than they used to be. Find a problem that people need solved that you have some expertise in and write a book about how to solve it. Writing a book is on many people's bucket lists, and now it's easier than ever to share your special gift of knowledge with others. Amazon Kindle will walk you through the process of uploading your book text once you're done, formatting your cover, and making a digital copy. Amazon KDP is the site you use to produce books.

Chapter 32 Help Students Write College Admissions Essays

Applying to and getting into college is a very stressful process. Parents and students are willing to pay for someone to review their essays and provide any fine-tuning necessary. This can make or break the admission process to a preferred university for a potential college student. Market to parents who want a second opinion on their child's college admissions essay. Upwork is a good resource for marketing this service or finding people who are looking for help.

Chapter 33 Online Surveys

Help companies improve their business by filling out surveys over the internet. The information you provide is stored in databases that are analyzed and helps provide statistical information for businesses. This data helps companies understand consumer behavior, increasing the functionality of their websites; making them easier to use by finding bugs in their platforms, and creating marketing programs for their customers. Websites such as Google Survey, Harris Poll Online, and MyPoints.com are some of the well-known and reliable survey sites. There are other sites that may have complaints against them. Before you invest too much time, read the reviews, do a trial, and see if they work for you: Survey Junkie, Swagbucks,

InboxDollars, OneOpinion, SurveyClub, VIP Voice, and GlobalTestMarket. The allure of being able to work from home or while traveling draws in many to the online survey business. It can be a very flexible option for work, just do your homework so you don't get suckered into doing work for free.

Chapter 34 Make an Audiobook

ACX helps you produce audiobooks which you can sell through Amazon, Audible, and iTunes. This is a good option if you're not into writing but want to create a book. You also have the option to become an audiobook reader. People send in 2–3-page scripts, and all you have to do is read them and send them back to the owner. If you get selected, you have the option to get paid fifty to two hundred dollars an hour or become a partner and receive a percentage of the audiobook sales.

Chapter 35 Shop for Food

People are working long hours, and they're trying to increase their productivity by outsourcing chores. You can help with food and grocery delivery services like InstaCart, Uber Eats, DoorDash, Postmates, or GrubHub. Customers go online and place grocery and food orders at their preferred stores, a personal shopper then goes to those stores and picks up the order the same day and delivers it to the customer. As a side benefit, you can also build up miles and rewards on your credit cards as you buy gas and shop for others.

A friend of mine makes over five thousand dollars a month doing grocery delivery. Her secret is to park outside Whole Foods Market or Costco, so she gets orders from wealthier customers, and so her tips end up being much higher.

Chapter 36 Become a Mystery Shopper

Companies, market research firms, and watchdog

organizations hire people to go into stores to gather data on the quality of service, compliance with regulations, or to gather information about services and products. The company you work for will pay you to go into a business anonymously and try out the products or services they offer. Once you're done, you'll give your opinion to help them improve their customer experience. These are some of the top websites through which you can sign up: Market Force, BestMark, Sinclair Customer Metrics, and IntelliShop.

Chapter 37 Use the Honey Chrome Extension When You Shop

The Honey Chrome extension helps you make money by saving money. It attaches to your Google Chrome, and as you shop online, it automatically finds the Internet's best coupon codes for you, so you don't have to try finding them yourself. An icon will pop up that you click on, and it will apply the coupon to your purchase.

Chapter 38 Sites That Get You Cash Back from Your Shopping

Swagbucks helps you earn gift cards by watching videos, filling out surveys, playing video games, shopping through their site, using their search engine, try samples, or check out offers. Rakuten Rewards gets a commission for sending you to partner websites to shop and shares the commission with you. The downside to these applications is they can cause you to buy things you don't need, so you end up spending dollars to earn pennies. So be wise when using these applications and don't allow them to influence your buying habits.

Chapter 39 Get Money Back from Online Purchases as the Price Drops Using Paribus

First, you shop online and save the email receipts from purchases. Paribus tracks your confirmation emails and monitors price changes. When the price changes, Paribus will notify you and help you get your money back.

Chapter 40 Cash Back with Dosh

With Dosh, you connect your debit and credit cards to your account, so whenever you shop at a partner location, it deposits cash from your purchases to your Dosh account. The money can then be transferred to your PayPal, bank account, or donated to a charity. You also get eight dollars for every friend you refer.

Chapter 41 Earn Cash with Ibotta or Drop

Both apps help you earn money back for buying certain groceries and brand specific items. Ibotta asks you to pick items from their grocery list to buy. You submit a picture of the receipt after you purchase the item and get paid with gift cards or cash via Venmo or PayPal. They also offer a ten-dollar bonus for new enrollees. This is modern day couponing, but with your smartphone.

Chapter 42 Free Money with CoinOut

Just take a picture of any receipt, from any retailer, and you'll get paid. I tried this, and I would get five cents to fifteen cents per receipt. This company gathers market research on your spending patterns so they can sell it to other companies which helps them spend their marketing dollars efficiently.

Chapter 43 Get Paid for Walking into Stores with Shopkick

You will earn points for walking into stores, scanning items, and for buying specific items indicated by the application. You get paid with gift cards. If you don't have a lot of self-control in stores, don't use this; it'll just end up costing you money instead of helping you earn some.

Chapter 44 Get Paid with the Toluna ShopTracker App

The Toluna ShopTracker App is operated by The

Harris Poll, a survey company that measures U.S. public opinion. It tracks your shopping habits for market research companies. They start you off with $3 for installing the app. Data is precious, and companies are willing to pay to get as much consumer information as they can so they can focus their marketing plans on people who will use their products. This type of apps simply gathers information on your habits, so the data can be sold to large companies.

Chapter 45 Buy and Sell Art

Investing in art is very popular amongst the wealthy because it is a "value-preserving asset class" with a lower call risk than assets priced daily, such as securities. The global art market is worth over 70 billion dollars, and there are over 40 million transactions in art a year. Therefore, if you have an art background, there are ample opportunities in the art market for you. If you do not have the funds to buy and sell art for yourself, you can do it for someone else or by connecting buyers and sellers and earning a commission.

Chapter 46 Flip Furniture from Home

Shop garage sales and thrift stores for antiques, refurbish, and resell them on eBay, Craigslist, and OfferUp.

I had a friend named Don who would rent a large van, drive state to state and fill it up with vintage furniture, then drive them home to Los Angeles where he would refurbish and sell them. He became a multimillionaire flipping furniture.

Chapter 47 Sell Used Books

My neighbor makes a living buying used books from thrift stores and selling them online and at swap meets. You can also comb through stores and enter the titles into online marketplaces to see their value. My neighbor says he often finds books worth a few hundred dollars for sale for $.10. You can also sell your books on SellBackYourBook.com, Amazon, or using my favorite app BookScouter. The Bookscouter app allows you to go into a thrift store or any other discount book location and scan the book's ISBN with the app, and it gives you the book's price recommendations, vendor reviews, and buyback resources.

Chapter 48 Buying and Selling Gift Cards

I buy gift cards for gas, Costco, supermarkets, or other necessities, and if I see a good deal, I buy and resell for more. Sometimes I find folks who need cash in a hurry, and they'll sell their gift cards for around fifty percent off face value. Good places to look for and sell gift cards are Craigslist, Cardpool, OfferUp, Facebook Marketplace, or Raise.

Chapter 49 Trading Sport Cards

In the '80s and '90s, I use to collect sports cards with my friends. On the weekends, we would make money going to card shows to buy and sell sports cards. Many of those friends have sold those cards and made huge profits one even bought a house with cards he had purchased back then with his lunch money. Sports card investing is now hitting full stride with the internet because sports card investing has demonstrated extremely impressive traders' returns. Like art, you have to know something about the industry or at least hire someone who knows. Otherwise, you'll have a hard time picking cards that will eventually be worth a great deal, some in the millions.

Chapter 50 Buying and Selling Cars

A friend of mine named Bagga Wilson taught me how to make up to twenty thousand a month working part time buying and selling cars. We used online used car websites such as auctions, Cars.com, Craigslist, Autotrader, OfferUp, etc. We focused on a few makes and models at a time. I scanned the sites until I found outliers in the low-price range. Some had a low price due to obvious reasons; body damage, high mileage, lost paperwork, etc. And some were sold by people who were getting divorced, moving, needed money quick, or only wanted to get rid of the car. Some cars had minor damage that was inexpensive to fix, but folks overestimated the cost of repairs needed or didn't want to dedicate the time to fix them. You have to run fast and have cash ready, or the vehicles will sell before you can get to them. Buy it low, clean it up, and relist the car at a mid-range price and on more websites. We recommend the internet because you'll get people from all over the country and even the world buying and having the car shipped which is much lower than it used to be. I often bought cars from other states if the price was right. Just be careful with scammers trying to send you fake checks, money orders, and money transfers.

Chapter 51 Vending Machines

Although some people make millions off vending machines, you're more likely to see a few well-placed machines generate residual income. The average person spends around $27 per year on products from vending machines. The average transaction costs $1.71, and a typical vending machine generates over $75 of revenue each week and over $300 per month. The more well-placed, well-stocked machines an owner operates, the greater their revenue and profits. Make sure to listen to customer wants and offer refunds whenever there is an issue to avoid losing repeat customers, who'll make up most of your customers.

Chapter 52 Print on Demand Products

Recently we were evaluating a new tenant for a rental unit, and as part of the rental process, she had to explain what the source of her income was. She made a living printing logos on cups, t-shirts, calendars, etc., and had over $500,000 in her bank account to back up her $600,000 a year income.

There are multiple websites online or brick and mortar establishments to help you start selling branded merchandise. One of the easiest to use is Merch by Amazon, which enables you to sell branded products designed by you and made, sold, and shipped by Amazon. There is no risk to you since there are no out-of-pocket costs to you. Teespring is a print-on-demand t-shirt website where you can custom-design your shirts and sell them through the site. Another website is Printful, which has hundreds of print-on-demand products and lets you syndicate your listings to Etsy and other stores.

Chapter 53 Auctions for other Peoples' Belongings

There is excess, left behind, or discontinued items in every industry. You can buy these items in bulk at auctions for reselling online or in person. UPS and other mail carriers sell unclaimed bundles of packages, the airlines' auction off luggage, and storage businesses will sell off storage units' contents. Once you receive your bulk purchase, the fun begins of opening packages and seeing what unclaimed surprises you might find.

Chapter 54 Sell White Labeled Products

As an entrepreneur, your first thought may be to try do-it-yourself. However, in many cases, building a customized product from scratch can set you up for failure. Doing things on your own will make you waste time, money, higher risk, and miss out on tools and solutions that already exist.

Many of these challenges can be avoided with a white label solution. "White label" is a fully supported product or service that's made by one company but sold by another—for example, the store brand foods at the market. You can purchase white label products and services from a company without branding. That way, you can focus on marketing and customizing the product with your logo, brand, and identity, allowing customers to associate the product with you. Meanwhile, the manufacturer can cost-effectively research and develop the product without concern for its marketing.

Supplements, skincare products, services, clothing, or food products are just some businesses you can start through white labeling. Consider what type of product you would like to make, then google, white labeling with that product or service, and get information from the companies. There is a full spectrum of services available. From designing your formula, a laboratory making your product, labeling, packing, and even shipping to the customer. You only have to come up with a concept, and the white labeler can do the rest for you, then you can pick up some of or all of the steps as you scale and build expertise.

Chapter 55 Sell on eBay, Amazon, and Other Online Stores

There are two types of arbitrage, the first is online arbitrage which is finding items for sale that have a spread which is a lower price on one website than relisting it on another site at a higher price. That spread is your potential profit. For example, buying a Black & Decker toaster on Target.com for $8.00, but seeing it for sale on Amazon.com for $20.00. So you relist it on Amazon for $19.90 so your price is the lowest and it sells, and you make $11.90 in profit. When someone buys the product you have listed, you drop ship the item to the customer. Drop shipping is when you sell the item, the item is then shipped directly from one website to the buyer from the other website. This saves you a lot of time and money as many people get Amazon Prime or other accounts that give you free shipping, which offers free shipping on all purchases.

This technique is very easy, and it has made countless millionaires. When you buy something on the internet, it's common to buy from one website and then receive the package from another website. This happens because you bought something that someone had found on one website and relisted on another, which can seem confusing if you don't understand what's going on. I had an issue with an item that was not the seller's fault, but I needed to return the item. When I contacted the seller, I was surprised to find that there were several sellers in other countries, such as Brazil, India and Egypt. These were folks relisting items they were finding on the internet that had a profitable spread. Then, when I purchased the product, it was drop shipped to me from a warehouse in the USA.

Some friends of mine started doing this when they were in Iraq and had lots of free time on base. When they came back to the States, they continued, and have made millions doing online arbitrage.

The second type is retail arbitrage, where you go into brick-and-mortar stores like Walmart, dollar stores, Target, or other major retailers and look for items they carry that have a favorable spread with an online retailer like eBay or Amazon. Amazon even has a smartphone application called Amazon Seller, that you can scan product barcodes while you're in the store, and it will give you the high and low price on Amazon, along with lots of information including how long it should take to sell the item. So, you can figure out exactly how much money you would make and how long it would take you to make it. You can also comb Craigslist, thrift stores, or garage sales for things that could sell for more on eBay or Amazon.

I have been very successful with retail arbitrage, especially around Christmas time. I'll comb the web for the hottest Christmas items, then search those items till I discover a spread in the prices. For example, one year a Tickle Me Elmo came out that was selling in stores for around forty dollars, but there was so much demand that the stores ran out of stock as everybody wanted this toy for their kids. Because it was the most sought-after toy that holiday, I was able to get over five hundred dollars for each Elmo and had a huge waiting list of people bidding the prices up even higher. I drove around and figured out delivery dates at Targets, Walmart, and other big stores around me that were selling them. I'd make a calendar and I'd do my rounds to those stores buying as many as I could. Oftentimes, when there was such high demand, the stores would set a limit as to how many of the particular items you could buy. To get around the purchase limit, I would bring my parents, girlfriend, and friends, and I'd pay them a commission for helping me buy the items. Some of my friends have made over twenty thousand during some holiday seasons selling toys, game consoles, and whatever the other must-have items were that holiday.

Chapter 56 Buy Used Items to Save on Retail Costs

When you need to purchase something, look on Craigslist, OfferUp, and eBay to see if you can find it there first at a lower price second hand. I've bought kayaks, skis, cameras, appliances, furniture, computers, food; just about anything you can think of from those sites. I've met people who had to move out of state and just wanted to sell as much as they could quickly, so they could save on moving costs and be on their way. I bought shower curtains, food, linens, potted plants, curtains, kitchen goods, everything I could possibly use in my Airbnb rentals or to simply upgrade my house.

Once I had to rent a U-Haul truck as one guy I met on Craigslist offered me everything in his house except his clothes for five hundred dollars. I emptied out his house of over thirty thousand dollars' worth of modern furniture, art, rugs, exotic plants, door mats, beds, toiletries, and even cleaning supplies. He even wanted to give me some broken down cars for free, but I just didn't have enough room to take it all. The gentleman was getting ready to rebuild a bigger house and didn't feel like moving anything. Had I not purchased the items, he said he would have just left them in the house and let the bulldozers knock down the house and dump everything into dumpsters. He said he was very grateful that I was helping him recycle.

Chapter 57 Look for Valuable Rewards Programs

Most rewards programs are a waste of time and meant to make you buy things you don't need; that's why I generally avoid grocery coupons. They typically promote unhealthy processed foods, so you suffer from collateral damage for saving a few bucks. My friend John Sendrey taught me to be curious, as sometimes programs could be very generous and help you generate revenue. We found a CVS Pharmacy deal using their Extra Care Bucks program that helped make over ten thousand dollars a month for several months until the program ended.

Another time during the holiday season, Albertsons grocery store chain had a deal going on to help sell gift cards during the holidays. They offered a thirty-dollar store credit for everyone hundred in gift cards we bought. On the surface, this seemed like a lousy deal for unhealthy fast food gift cards. However, after a review, we found that we could buy one hundred dollars in gasoline gift cards which we would be using throughout the year anyway and use my rewards credit cards that gave me five percent more back for everyone hundred I spent at grocery stores. We ended up buying as many as I could, which was twenty thousand dollars' worth of gasoline cards that I used up in a year, and that I was going to have to buy anyway, six thousand dollars' worth of free groceries and one thousand dollars cash back on my credit card. In one month, we made seven thousand dollars profit on a twenty thousand investment on necessities.

Another strategy is to get a permanent ink pen and write the percentage for each type of reward on the credit cards you have. For example, on my Citibank card, I have 5% gas, 3% restaurant, 2% all others, or on my Bank of America card 4% groceries, 3% gas, 1% all others. When I'm about to make a purchase, I look for the card that gives me the highest reward for each type of purchase. For example, when I'm going to buy gas, I only use my Citibank card because it gives me 5% back, but if I'm grocery shopping, I'd use my Bank of America card, because it gives me 4% instead of the 2% I would get with my Citibank card.

Chapter 58 Look for Ways to Save on Outings

When you want to go out, shop StubHub, SeatGuru, or Travelzoo and see what's on sale. There was a Bruno Mars concert in Los Angeles, and the cheapest ticket was $150. Katy Perry was also performing that night, so I was able to get tickets for $10 instead of the usual one hundred. When it rains or there is unfavorable weather, you can get good last-minute deals on sporting events and concerts. You can also check for sites that have lists of free outings near you and free museum nights.

Chapter 59 Pool Cleaning Service

A pool, spa, or hot tub cleaning business is an excellent way to start a business with residual income. Once you get clients, most people forgot about you and send you payment every month if you do a good job. A pool cleaner visits a client's business (apartments, hotels, gyms, etc.) or home to maintain the water's chemical balance, clean the filters and pumps, clean, and check the skimmers. A weekly or bi-monthly schedule is typical unless there is a storm or there is high usage.

Investing time in an apprenticeship, learning legal requirements, health codes, and becoming knowledgeable about environmentally friendly products, can help you differentiate and grow your pool cleaning business. Professional pool cleaners can make $50 to $60 per hour and up to $200 if they do equipment maintenance or repair.

Chapter 60 Help People Get Things Done Around Their House

Help people with services such as moving items, handyman jobs, organization, assembling furniture, cleaning, yard work, pickup and delivery, gardening, washing windows, removing snow, moving and packing, and much more. TaskRabbit, Craigslist, and TakL allow you to list your services and get gigs from an hour to a full day's work whenever you need the hours. My friend discovered a niche unclogging toilets as most people don't like this kind of dirty work. He charges $125 a visit for about ten minutes work, and he makes a living off this using a $40 toilet auger he bought from Home Depot.

Chapter 61 Babysitting

You can offer your services by setting up a profile through Sittercity.com or Care.com, and they'll connect you with families in your area. This is an easy way to make some extra cash a few nights a week, but be careful, folks can be touchy with their kids.

Chapter 62 Care for Pets

As more and more people are choosing to stay single and not have kids, pets are becoming surrogate children. Three-quarters of Americans in their thirties have dogs and fifty-one percent have cats. Overall, in the USA, fifty percent of people have dogs and thirty-five percent have cats. Pets are becoming a replacement for children and the multibillion-dollar pet industry has lots of niches to work in. You can walk dogs, offer daycare, grooming, boarding, house sit pets, host pet birthday parties, or do drop-in visits to pets in their homes while folks are on vacation or at work. Sites such as Wag! and Rover.com offer you a variety of ways to help people care for their pets. My family and I once made eight thousand dollars in one-month pet sitting through these sites.

As an add-on business, you can start a business as a dog groomer or a dog trainer and offer these services to your clients or advertise them separately. This is a business with lots of potential for growth. Most of the pets can be a joy to be around, especially since most of them are well cared for and have been trained. However, just like people, pets can have off days, get into fights with one another, chew and damage your property, escape into your neighborhood, get ill, and even get homesick. Therefore, this work is for people who spend a lot of time at home. It's best to do when you have a work-from-home job or are home studying for school.

Chapter 63 Pet Waste Cleanup

Busy pet owners are outsourcing their pet waste cleanup and removal duties. Many additional services are also available such as yard odor eliminator and disinfectant, deck and patio spray downs, and flea and tick spray downs. Websites such as DoodyCalls, Pet Butler, and poop911 can help you add hundreds extra per week in recurring clients.

Chapter 64 Aquarium Maintenance

Some aquarium owners hire aquarium maintenance professionals to clean and maintain their aquariums. You can either work from home, give commissions for referrals, or rent space in a pet store.

The start-up costs are low. You'll need basic supplies such as buckets, water changing tubes, faucet adaptors, and chemicals to balance the water chemistry. Your operations base will likely be your home and the vehicle you use to travel to your clients.

Scheduling is very flexible, and you can work as much or as little as you want. There are opportunities for expansion into many areas, such as aquarium setup or selling aquarium supplies to your clients. Clients can range from businesses to private homes.

Chapter 65 Pond Maintenance

Although pond maintenance is very similar to aquarium maintenance, the work is slightly different and requires a different skill set. Pond maintenance requires knowledge of local wildlife so you can protect pond fish from being eaten, gardening, maintaining chemicals, landscaping, which is typically outdoors, and dredging services. The work is typically more frequent than aquarium maintenance since the ponds are usually outside and exposed to the elements.

Chapter 66 Become a House Sitter

You can get paid to watch people's homes, gardens, and pets while they travel or work. As a bonus, you can live rent free staying at people's homes who want someone to stay the night there to watch over their property. My friend signed up for this service and would take on several assignments at the same time. After his day job, he would drive his route visiting the homes he had agreed to drop in on, and then spend the night at the house he had agreed to spend the night at. You can sign up to be a house sitter at HouseSitter.com, TrustedHousesitters, Nomador, HouseCarers, and HouseSit Match.

Chapter 67 Driving Instructor

Due to budget cuts, most high schools no longer offer driver's education to students. Unlicensed drivers now must find private driver's education to become a licensed driver. To become a driving instructor, you must be 21 years old, be a high school graduate, have a clean driving record, take a physical, get fingerprinted, pass an exam, pay a state licensing fee to the department of motor vehicles (DMV). These requirements vary by country, but the demand for driving instructors exists in all of them. You can work for someone else or yourself advertising your services offline and online as a driving instructor.

Chapter 68 Become A Driver

By signing up for Uber or Lyft, you can work whenever you have free time giving people rides. If you already have a job, then set your worksite as your destination and your home as the destination on the way home from your worksite. This option allows you to give people rides on your way to and from work each day, helping you generate extra revenue without very much effort. You can also drive during peak times and get bonuses for driving on holidays.

A few people I see driving for these rideshare services have new cars. Definitely, use the oldest and most efficient model car. I can't think of anyone who has turned down a ride because they didn't like the car they were being picked up in.

Chapter 69 Rent Your Car

My buddy bought a nice sports car, and by renting it for a few days a week, the car ended up being free. You can list your vehicle on websites such as Turo, Getaround, Maven, and drivecanvas.com. You decide how often you want to loan your car out, how much you want to charge for someone else to use it, and the service provides you with liability insurance for your car if you use their platform. It's basically a car rental platform for people to rent out their own cars. Some have the option for you to rent your car for certain hours of the day. For example, while you're at work and not using the car or after you're home for the night.

Chapter 70 Mobile Mechanic

Most people taking a day off from work to have their car worked on can cause a significant loss of income and productivity. Save people time and hassle by bringing the shop and services to them. You can try TaskRabbit, craigslist.org, or YourMechanic.com to advertise your services, then travel to people's homes or offices to service their car. YourMechanic.com has everything well organized for scheduling, pricing, booking appointments, payments, accessing service history, and maintenance reminders.

Chapter 71 Mobile Car Wash and Detailing

Providing a mobile car wash and detailing service is another way to save people time, hassle and increase their productivity. By providing convenience and time saving, you're able to build repeat business with low start-up costs, flexibility, and you can get clients in batches at schools, worksites, office parks, sporting events, shopping malls, and large parking lots.

Chapter 72 Window Cleaning

Window cleaners clean the windows and glass surfaces of residential and commercial buildings. They typically use glass-cleaning solutions, clothes, squeegee blades, and water to remove grime and operate lift equipment to access hard-to-reach windows. Window cleaning requires minimal startup capital, compensation can be $50 to $70 per hour, and the scheduling is flexible.

Chapter 73 Floor Cleaning

Polishing floors or cleaning carpets is a tedious task that most people would like to avoid since it takes coordination to move all of the furniture and scrub the floors till they're clean. Presenting an opportunity to build a client base on a recurring monthly or annual basis to help offices and private spaces look their best.

Chapter 74 Mobile Laundry Service

Washing, folding, and ironing clothes is the least desirable of people's household chores. Most people let their clothes build up until the task becomes time-consuming and prefer to outsource the job to someone else. Laundry service has little start-up costs, flexibility, and is an excellent way to catch up on some reading or studying. As word gets around about your quality service, it's easy to add more recurring customers.

Chapter 75 Clean People's Homes

When I was a teenager my mom taught me and my older brother Bobby how to clean people's homes. I used to enjoy seeing people come home to their tidy house and start smiling when they saw how nice everything looked. But one of the best parts was learning about how other people live. We worked for writers, actors, millionaires, billionaires, porn stars, professional athletes, professors, and everything else you can think of. Because cleaning someone's home can be an intimate experience, you sort of become part of the family. This experience gave my brother and me exposure to how other people think, live, and see the world.

Housekeeper.com allows you to post jobs and look for jobs cleaning people's homes in your neighborhood. The pay is good, the schedules are very flexible, and people really appreciate your work.

Chapter 76 Commercial Cleaning Service

Two of my friends have become millionaires offering cleaning services to businesses, banks, gyms, movie theaters, and office buildings after hours.

Every business you can think of needs to be cleaned, and if you are willing to work at night and during off-hours, the opportunities are abundant. A commercial cleaning business requires little overhead, is flexible, and anyone can start one since there is so much demand.

Chapter 77 Become A Personal Chef

Hiring a personal chef is not only for wealthy people anymore. People are getting busier and it's becoming more of a challenge for them to find time to cook for themselves and eat healthy. This has caused an explosion in the prepackaged meal market. But nothing beats a fresh home-cooked meal. The website HireAChef.com allows you to connect with people in your area, who would like to have a private chef for an event or on an ongoing basis. My friend has a private chef who stops by his house twice a week and cooks all the meals he needs for three or four days at a time and leaves everything packaged. So all he has to do is take the food out of the refrigerator, take it to work or heat it up. She has a list of his likes and dislikes, and before she starts over every few days, she will make a stop at the market and pick up what she needs to prepare the menu she has selected for the next few days. Apparently, she has several private clients and spends her days driving from house to house preparing meals for other people as well. My friend has lost a lot of weight, improved his health, and he says he is saving money not going out to restaurants anymore.

Chapter 78 Mobile Hairstylist

A mobile hairstylist travels from client to client, usually to their homes, to provide services they typically get from a hairstylist in a salon. Most mobile hairstylists' duties include offering a color, cut, or style, either for routine hair care or special occasions. Nursing homes and other places where large groups of people live often award the right to see all of their residents to one mobile hairstylist to meet the needs of people with limited mobility.

Chapter 79 Become a Personal Wardrobe Consultant

A stylist or consultant will examine your wardrobe over video conference calls or in person at your home. They figure out what would work well with you and what does not work well with you. They help you save money by helping you select clothing that looks good on you according to your skin color, hair color, and body type. They will also teach you how to put outfits together and look your best for meetings, events, and special occasions. Think of the cable television show *Queer Eye for the Straight Guy*.

List your services on Upwork, Craigslist, and Indeed to become a private wardrobe consultant and help others look their best. You can also list a variety of other services, such as nutritional consulting, massage, dog services, handyman, personal training, wedding services, life coaching, hypnotherapy, etc.

Chapter 80 Participate in Clinical Trials

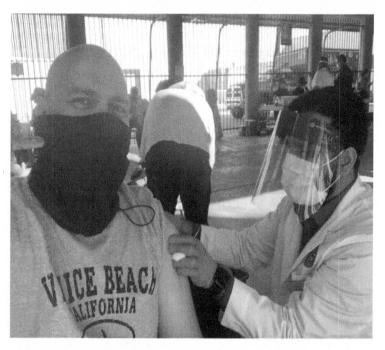

ClinicalTrials.gov allows you to participate in an assortment of trials to generate revenue by renting out your body for experiments. You can also join in paid research studies at your local university and focus groups through Find Focus Groups and FocusGroup.com.

I used to participate in these trials when I was in college, and I never felt like I was in any kind of danger. In fact, they are highly regulated, and you can have some exciting experiences completing the assignments. Clinical trials are usually drug or illness related where focus groups respond to questionnaires pertaining to specific topics.

Chapter 81 Get Paid to Stay in Bed

NASA will pay you $18,000 to lie in bed for 70 days as part of a study. Check out NASA IRB. The catch is you have to do everything lying down, eating, drinking, watching movies, playing video games, reading, and even showering. I thought about doing this so I can have time to write more books, but the truth is, lying in bed for such a prolonged period could cause long term muscle and nerve damage. You may be able to recover most of it as long as you do an extensive exercise program after the two months.

Chapter 82 Participate in Psychological Studies

Complete paid psychological studies. Most universities keep a database of current studies you can join. These are generally lower risk and require a shorter time commitment. At the university I attended, they had hundreds of these experiments going on at the same time. I could walk into the psychology building and scan through catalogs full of studies with short descriptions. The description indicated how long the tests usually lasted, what was involved, and how much they paid.

Chapter 83 Telecommute

FlexJobs, Indeed, and ZipRecruiter have listings for telecommute jobs; you can access remotely part-time, freelance, and flexible jobs that fit your schedule. These are great options if you have a family or like to travel. I was offered a job as an insurance reviewer, and as long as I kept my residency in my home state, I could travel and work at the same time.

Chapter 84 Complete Micro Jobs

Micro jobs are all kinds of temporary, task-type jobs. Amazon MTurk, Clickworker, ClixSense, EasyShift, Figure Eight, UserTesting, Field Agent, Gigwalk, Quicktate, iDictate, The Smart Crowd, Scribie, TryMyUI, and Skyword allow you to complete micro jobs or pieces of larger jobs and get paid. The variety of micro jobs are endless. There are micro jobs for all types of budgets and skill sets.

Chapter 85 Buy and Sell Domain Names

You try to anticipate domain names that might become useful by searching for popular phrases on the

Internet. Based on that information you buy them, and then put them up for sale for more. It's almost like purchasing a stock that could become valuable in the future.

I have a friend that follows politics and buys domain names based on how who he thinks might run for office, i.e. Bush/Cheney.com etc.

Chapter 86 Buy Successful Websites

By buying an existing site, you're purchasing an established concept that has already proven itself to be profitable. With an established website, you won't have to make the site profitable because you'll be getting the income from day one. If you have funds to invest, buying a pre-existing cash flow business and building it up even further is the fastest path to a new business.

Chapter 87 Build Sales with ClickFunnels

ClickFunnels is a one-stop platform that streamlines the process of integrating websites to help you sell more and market your products. If you already have a website or want to start one, this site offers everything you need to build and run your website. It simplifies the process by giving you everything you need to sell, market, and deliver the services and products online without hiring anyone else. Cutting your costs, making it easier, and saving you time.

Chapter 88 Do Email Marketing

Once you attract subscribers to your blog or website, you can start making money by using email marketing platforms like Leadpages, Constant Contact, AWeber, and ConvertKit. These websites help you keep track of people visiting your site so you can send them marketing materials from your business or from other people's businesses. It will help you sell your products and make a profit or get paid to market other people's products and get a commission off the sale of their products.

Chapter 89 Start a Podcast

If you're not into writing, you can start a podcast instead. Record yourself talking and publish your audio recording. As people subscribe to your podcast and as your audience grows, you'll get sponsorships. Podcast listening is growing exponentially, and currently, there are over 112 million listeners. There are about one million podcasters versus five hundred million YouTube producers. Therefore, this is a market to start learning as there is a lot of growth potential and opportunity to build revenue. The flexibility is excellent, as you can produce your podcast from just about anywhere. I listen to podcasts from expats who live in other countries and give interesting advice about relocating to and living in those countries, and how to thrive there. You can learn a lot from people who post podcasts; they have up-to-the-minute information from people who are actually doing what they are talking about.

Chapter 90 Work at a Startup

If you'd like to start your own startup, this is a good way to get your bearings by working for a startup and learning how they operate. This will help you learn the business and get valuable experience. AngelList has listings for all types of positions working at startups.

My neighbor Ryan has a bachelor's degree and took a break from his master's in business administration (MBA) program to work for an electric scooter startup. He had the opportunity to work for two other startups before this one, and he says the experience has changed his professional life. All of Ryan's startup jobs have paid him minimum wage. You may ask why someone with a college degree would want a minimum wage job? There are many reasons to love working for startups; more opportunities, more responsibilities, learning different aspects of the business, working with and learning from innovators, you'll have to work hard, you learn to be self-sustainable, and you'll learn to survive on little. If you can take a long-term view of working for a startup, you can make much more in the long run.

At Ryan's last startup, he was given a 0.5% ownership stake in the company. The company recently had several rounds of investing, and although he makes minimum wage, his 0.5% stake is worth over $200,000 even though he's only worked for the company a little over two years. Aside from the valuable experience and knowledge you gain the ownership stakes can be worth a fortune. The startup business is such a huge business that 30% of all of the money invested in the USA is invested in the bay area where most of the tech companies are located. In fact, more money is invested in the bay area than in New York, Los Angeles, and Boston combined. Taking a short term pay cut to gain access to this large market could be worth a lot more in the long run.

Chapter 91 Become a Search Engine Evaluator

Appen has work from home opportunities for people to research, evaluate, and give feedback on search engine results using techniques provided by the company. Basically, they want to make sure that the search engine results are relevant to the keywords that people are researching. This helps to ensure that the quality of the information that people are finding is related to what they actually are looking for.

Chapter 92 Make Money with Affiliate Marketing

Make a blog or YouTube channel and grow your audience. As your channel grows, companies will want to partner up to advertise and sell their product on your site. When people buy the merchants' products through your site, you get paid a commission. This type of business model is earning lots of people up to millions per month.

Amazon affiliate links are amongst the simplest to use. Amazon pays you 5–10% of every purchase your readers make for Amazon products. Amazon links are inexpensive, simple, and you can create your account in less than 5 minutes. These links are 100% passive income. You can also insert these links to all your content, your services, your coaching, courses, and emails.

Chapter 93 Computer Repair

YouTube videos can help you fix over ninety percent of hardware and software problems with tablets, computers, and cell phones. There are also more of these devices in the USA than there are people, so there are ample business opportunities. More elaborate and complicated repairs will require an investment in hardware, tools, software, and supplies, but you can subcontract this work or charge more to repair serious issues.

Most people don't even try to fix their electronics. They buy a new one instead of fixing the one they have. Therefore, there is a large market for offering computer setup, salvaging electronics, selling them, and retrieving valuable computer data.

Chapter 94 Work for the Largest Tech Companies in the World

Large technology companies are starving for trained staff who can do the work they need to stay in business. So much that the USA imports over 400,000 foreign workers a year to meet the minimum needs. If there weren't government caps, American companies would import several million workers. If you're reading this book, you're probably looking for a way to get a high paying job, and this is the ultimate way to achieve that goal quickly. As always, necessity breeds ingenuity, and multiple universities and websites funded by tech billionaires like Bill Gates have started offering free education online to help meet some of the needs. Not having money for college is no longer an excuse; you can work for Google, Apple, and other big tech companies by learning skills in high demand subjects in hours, rather than spending years in college. Allowing you to earn a six-figure income by taking free classes. Get training in areas of high demand through;

1. Stanford Online

Stanford University offers free online courses in executive education, professional certificates, and advanced degrees. Stanford Online offers courses from their undergraduate and graduate schools, including Stanford Business School, Stanford Medical School, Stanford Law School, among others.

2. Codeacademy

Codeacademy is an interactive website that teaches you how to code in multiple programming languages. In less than 11 hours, you can complete most of the free courses. Codeacademy has trained over 45 million people in programming, web development, data science, and computer science. Codeacademy graduates work at Microsoft, Google, Instagram, Facebook, Bloomberg, and IBM, among other top companies.

3. TED-Ed

TED-Ed has a global network of over 250,000 teachers that serves millions of teachers and students worldwide every week. TED-Ed includes creative content such as original animated videos and a platform for teachers to create interactive lessons.

4. Khan Academy

Khan Academy is free for teachers, students, and offers lessons for students from kindergarten through early college. Class available include science, math, technology, grammar, business, science, history, engineering, SAT®, AP® exams, and more. Khan Academy's founders include Bill and Melinda Gates Foundation, Ann & Jon Doerr, Reed Hastings, and Google.

5. Coursera

Coursera has more than 35 million students, 2,700

courses, 150 university partners, 250 specializations, and four degrees. Aside from free content, Coursera offers courses ranging from $29 - $99. Degrees and specializations are higher priced. Instructors include experts from the world's top universities and colleges, including recorded video lectures, community discussion forums, and peer-reviewed and graded coursework. You can receive a course certificate for each course you complete.

6. edX

Founded by MIT and Harvard, edX is a global non-profit seeking to remove three traditional education barriers: location, cost, and access. edX has more than 2,400 courses and 20 million learners from world-class universities. In addition to free classes, edX also offers courses for a fee.

7. Udemy

Udemy, a global education marketplace, has 30 million students, 100,000 courses in 50 languages, 42,000 instructors, and 22 million video instruction minutes. Unlike other online education platforms driven by content from colleges and universities, Udemy allows content creators to curate their courses and teach them online.

Chapter 95 Test Websites and Applications

WhatUsersDo, Enroll, Userfeel.com, TryMyUI, and Analysia.com allow you to test out websites and apps for about 15-20 minutes each, and pay around ten dollars per test. AppKarma pays you with PayPal and gift cards for trying out apps. As you try out the functions of the app and find issues or have suggestions for improvement, you report them to the company. This helps companies work out the bugs in their programs, saving them money and embarrassment.

Chapter 96 Develop an Application

Create an application for smartphones, based on something you believe could fill a niche or need for someone. If you're not sure how to make an application for your concept, and if you don't know how to make the application, you can hire someone on Upwork who does and have them help you build your application.

Chapter 97 Become a Freelance Developer

Most of the freelance sites previously mentioned also have work for developers, but these sites specialize in developer jobs: FreeLancer, Joomlancers, ProgrammerMeetDesigner, 10x Management, Gigster, YouTeam, Codeable, and Talent Cupboard. Software is highly scalable, so you can create something once and sell it over and over again. If you don't know how to write code, you can hire someone on these sites to build your computer program or application.

Chapter 98 Produce Your Own YouTube Channel

You can make videos about anything that interests you and post them on YouTube. YouTube is experiencing double-digit growth every year. Therefore, there is a huge market opening up for potential YouTubers. The barriers to entry are very low and the rewards can be in the millions. In newspapers, news channels and TV, we are starting to see news about YouTubers instead of just traditional celebrities. This is just some of the evidence of the growing clouds and influence in our society. It can be a great opportunity for someone to share their special skills with the world.

Chapter 99 Let Others Watch you Play Video Games

Twitch is a platform for live gameplay and commentary, talk shows, cooking shows, sporting events, and gaming conventions. Twitch streamers "broadcast" their gameplay or activity by sharing their screen with fans and subscribers who can hear and watch them live.

Twitch Partners earn money through affiliate programs, shares of ad revenue generated from their page, endorsement deals, and brand sponsorships. Expert streamers can make between $3,000 to $5,000 each month, playing around 40 hours a week. Ad revenue can fetch on average $250 for every 100 subscribers.

Chapter 100 Become a Social Media Influencer

You can get advertisers to pay you for marketing their products to your followers on Instagram, Twitter, or YouTube. This is a form of marketing where the company focuses its marketing efforts on an influential person rather than a target market as a whole. The influential person identified is then expected to market their product to their followers, therefore, exerting their influence over them in exchange for being paid marketing fees.

Chapter 101 Start a Social Media Marketing Business for Others

You can approach businesses and have them hire you to market their products or services using social media. You can do marketing with Facebook, YouTube, Instagram, and blogs for yourself and your customers, and charge them a marketing fee. There are also sites where you can market your marketing business; PeoplePerHour, Remotive, and Aquent.

Chapter 102 Set up a Fan Club

Instagram is the Pg-13 version of OnlyFans, where

content creators can earn money from users who subscribe to their content. Content creators can then receive funding directly from their fans every month through monthly subscriptions, tips, and pay-per-view services. It's like a private Instagram only for you and your followers. It is popular with sex workers, content creators in physical fitness, musicians, and other creators who post regularly online. People are attracted to OnlyFans for many reasons, from companionship, entertainment, and arousal. The highest-paid earners on OnlyFans are women.

Chapter 103 Join MobileXpression

This site tracks your internet usage on your tablet and smartphone. You earn gift cards for participating in their program, and they donate a tree on your behalf once you've been a member for at least ninety days. No real downside to this; you earn money for participating in their market research program.

Chapter 104 Donate Plasma

You can donate plasma up to three times a week for about fifty dollars per donation. Check out DonatingPlasma.org to find your nearest donation center. Giving blood and plasma are good for your health because it rids your body of older or damaged cells, forcing your body to generate new healthy cells during the recovery process. Donating can also reduce your harmful cholesterol levels.

Chapter 105 Donate Stool.

If you live in the Boston area, you can donate stool for forty dollars a specimen at OpenBiome.org. The stool is used as part of a fecal microbiota transplant (FMT), or a stool transplant. The fecal matter from a healthy person is transplanted via enema, colonoscopy, or stool infusion into another person who needs it. This process helps introduce healthy bacteria into the colon of the recipient.

Chapter 106 Women Can Donate Their Eggs

Women can donate their eggs to other women who do not produce healthy eggs, but who want to have children. The pay is around fourteen thousand dollars per donation; however, when I was a student at the University of Southern California (USC), I saw advertisements in the school paper offering up to one hundred thousand dollars per donation.

Chapter 107 Men Can Donate Sperm

Men can donate sperm for about one thousand five hundred a month depending on how often they make deposits. Check out SpermBankDirectory.com to find the closest sperm donation center. I tried this in college and only made it to the fourth page of a fifty-page questionnaire when I found out I couldn't make a donation because I was in my first year in a four-year university, and they didn't accept applicants until their second year.

Chapter 108 Donate Your Body After You Die

Donate your body to science, and you will get a free cremation when you pass away. Check out BioGift and Science Care. When I was in school, I had the opportunity to work on several of the corpses in my classes as part of my training. If it weren't for selfless people, we wouldn't have bodies for new medical staff to practice on and to conduct research.

Chapter 109 Manage Children's Online Learning

More and more students are learning online. Full K-12 and college degrees are now available online for free. Some parents are working and don't have the time to dedicate to managing their child's online education. These programs can replace or augment any educational program with courses in entrepreneurship, critical thinking, personal finance, and nutrition to supplement the traditional curriculum.

With parents working at home due to covid-19, you can interact with the student remotely or over the phone to complete course work in Khan Academy, Stanford online, Codecademy, or countless other free schools while parents are working in the room next door.

Chapter 110 Become a Tutor

Tutoring is growing and offers a variety of options for both tutors and students. You can make YouTube videos like the Khan Academy and make money on advertising. Or you can use websites such as Chegg ($20 an hour), Brainfuse 9$10-$15 an hour), Tutor.com ($9-$13 an hour), Skooli ($25 an hour), Yup ($10-$13), LandiEnglish.com ($18-$25), TutorMe ($18 an hour), and Elevate K-12 ($15 an hour). You have multiple options to meet people in person, video conference, or talk over the phone to help tutor students.

Chapter 111 Become an Online Music or Acting Teacher

Teach music or acting lessons over the internet using Lessonface, an online marketplace that connects students with highly qualified music and acting teachers who can teach online or in person. Instructors can make $60 or more per hour for individual lessons or much more for group lessons. All you need is a computer or tablet with a webcam and reliable Internet access.

Chapter 112 Become a Substitute Teacher

If you have at least a bachelor's degree, you can register to work as a substitute teacher for day or night school classes. Being a substitute teacher is a great way to pick up extra high paying work when you need it. And working with kids is fulfilling. Here in Los Angeles, I have several friends who substitute teach as they work to become actors, singers, or work towards other careers in the entertainment industry. After applying and being approved, you can look online and book yourself to work the same day if you like. You can also apply to several school districts, so you have more work options.

Chapter 113 Produce an Online Course

Udemy is an online marketing and marketplace that allows course creators to publish, promote, and sell their premade courses online. Teachable allows you to customize how your course will function and sell your courses through their website, but they do not market the courses for you.

One of the keys of this book is to find out what your areas of expertise are and leverage them as much as you can. Producing an online course is another option for leveraging that specialized knowledge that you might have. The fact is, that no matter how simple you think your skills may be, there is always someone out there that wants to learn it. So, if you can organize your information into an online course, you can market and sell it online through the marketplaces mentioned above.

Chapter 114 Teach ESL Online

On Qkids, you can sign up to teach English to children in China for about twenty dollars an hour. You get a lesson plan for the class, and all you do is guide the kids through the lesson in English. This is a growing field, as students in developing countries look for ways to build their competitive advantage by learning conversational English. This is helpful in international business as English is the most common language used in multinational business.

Chapter 115 Become a Personal Coach or Mentor

If you have specialized training or expertise in a specific area, you can use those skills to foster someone else's learning and get paid for it. First learn public speaking skills, volunteer so you can practice and build a name, and finally start offering your services for a price. You can market your speeches to organizations or institutions to build your brand and get experience. Being a motivational speaker is one of the highest demand and highest paid jobs available. Starting out as a coach or a mentor can be the start of a lucrative career. Think of Tony Robbins and all the positive change he's been able to cause in the world.

You may not think of yourself as a coach, but people aren't paying you for coaching, they're paying you for an outcome. If you can help get people from point A to B, you can make money coaching. Wherever you are in your experience, you know things others don't. In most cases, people don't care what degrees or credentials you have; they care if you can get them where they want to go.

Here is a simple way to get started.

1. Ask your readers to answer a one-question survey about your niche.

2. Compile the answers and find the core question.

3. Find the best solution to that question.

4. Make a sales page selling a coaching package that answers that core question.

As a beginner, one-hour dollars an hour is the standard rate that should be charged for a coaching package. These days, people are going to people they trust and know can solve their problems for an affordable price. People like you.

Chapter 116 Provide Doula Services

Doulas educate & prepare their clients for natural, unmedicated, medicated, vaginal, or surgical births. They're like a coach during child labor a doula provides emotional, practical, and informational support to their client(s), adapting to what is needed. The doula can offer help and suggestions on comfort measures such as breathing, relaxation, movement, and positioning.

Chapter 117 Carrying Someone Else's Baby In Your Womb

Become a surrogate mother carrying someone else's baby in your womb, known as gestational surrogacy. It pays around twenty-four to forty-five thousand dollars per pregnancy. Hollywood movie stars have made this practice popular amongst the rich and famous who often pay much more as long as you follow their guidelines which include eating very healthy food that they will provide. This saves the celebrity from the physical damage of the pregnancy and the recovery time which means they get to keep working and earning an income.

Chapter 118 Rent Yourself as a Friend

With RentAFriend.com, you can rent local friends from all over the world. You can contact a friend to go hiking, hang out with, catch a movie or have dinner with, or someone to go with you to a party or event. Rent a friend to teach you a new skill or hobby, or to show you around an unfamiliar town. RentaFriend.com facilitates (strictly platonic) paid companionship. It is not a dating website or an escort agency. Friends can make $20-50 an hour to hang out with new friends.

Chapter 119 Become a Professional Cuddler

Cuddling plays an essential role in our wellbeing; it's a natural antidepressant, strengthens our immune system, and helps decrease anxiety. Providing cuddle therapy is an excellent way to comfort, console, encourage, listen, and help people pursue positive emotions. Professional cuddlers can make from $40-100 an hour and several thousand a month. Check out websites such as cuddlist.com or CuddleComfort.

Chapter 120 Caregiver for Disabled Persons

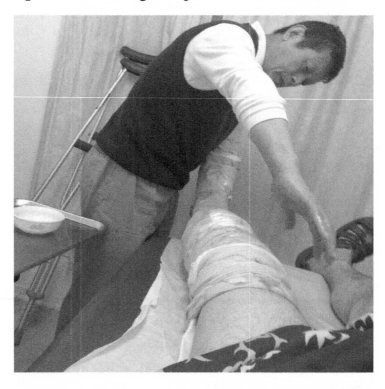

There are a variety of opportunities here. They vary from grocery shopping, driving to appointments, cleaning, cooking, and personal care. As the baby boomers age, there are a lot of openings for this kind of work. My grandmother, mother, and sister have provided assistance to disabled people. The work is personally rewarding. I once had a job where I got free rent and groceries. All I had to do was come to the person's home at night and sleep in a room of my own. He was independent but didn't want to sleep alone in the house at night.

Chapter 121 Become a Personal Trainer

Fueled by a 16% annual growth rate and an

increased demand for healthier living, there is a high demand for personal trainers. They can train people efficiently and safely to get them into better shape and live healthier lives. It only takes a few weeks to get certified, and you can start your own business training people in the gym, their homes, public spaces, or your home.

Chapter 122 Make Money Losing Weight

The website HealthyWage lets you bet on your weight loss. If you lose weight, then you make some extra money. My friend Richard loves to gamble, and happened to weigh over 400 lbs, so this concept was perfect for him. He joined and has been losing weight and winning money so it definitely works. It's been a win-win, although the website makes money relying on people not sticking to their weight loss plans and having to lose the money they wagered.

Chapter 123 Join Nielsen Digital Voice

You install their safe and secure Nielsen Digital Voice App on your smartphone, and it monitors how you use your phone. You earn rewards and get entry into their monthly $10,000 sweepstakes. A market research company is gathering your phone habits so they can resell the data to other companies. Generally harmless and allows you to earn some income.

Chapter 124 Become a Sports Referee

Recreational leagues need officials to officiate basketball, baseball, football, soccer, etc. and you get paid for doing so. My friend John is a soccer referee on weekends. He says his top reason for refereeing is exercise, and he gets to have some fun.

Chapter 125 Become a Bookkeeper

Learntobeabookkeeper.com teaches you how to launch a bookkeeping business that can pay about sixty dollars an hour. This is another good option if you want to stay at home with your family or travel and work. The job can be done anywhere you have an internet connection and a laptop.

Chapter 126 Get Paid to Watch Movie Previews

InboxDollars pays you to watch movies from playlists; you can earn over two hundred twenty-five dollars a month to do so. Market Force Information pays you thirty dollars to actually go to the theaters, watch movies, and fill out surveys about the film. This helps movie studios gather market data so they can adjust their marketing strategies.

Chapter 127 Master of Ceremony

An event host works at events, bars, or parties, getting people excited and prepared to have fun. A successful master of ceremonies can make an audience feel at ease, have strong time management skills, create a good atmosphere, and be skilled at public speaking. This job would be well-suited to people who enjoy entertaining and have a good sense of humor.

Chapter 128 Event Card Dealer

Professional card dealers go to dealer school and work in casinos. But many people have their poker nights and card games at parties and other private events and need a dealer. Learn table games such as poker and blackjack, physically deal cards, track bets, understand who has won the game or hand, and how much each player has won or lost. A neutral third party can help keep the peace amongst friends.

Chapter 129 Online Casino Promotion Hunter

Gambling is not a fair investment strategy, but you don't have to be good at it to take advantage of promotions. Online casinos offer bonuses if you deposit a dollar amount and pay you a percentage of 100-500% of your initial deposit to try out their service and give them the chance to get you hooked. The key is to make money fast and cash out once you've bet the bonus and your deposit a certain number of times per the bonus agreement.

Chapter 130 Get Free Lottery Tickets

Lucktastic is an app that gets you free scratchers that can earn you gift cards and instant wins from one dollar to ten thousand dollars. Something good to try while you're waiting in line or trying to kill a few minutes. Otherwise, you're better off reading a book or listening to NPR if you have some free time.

Chapter 131 Earn Rewards for Donating

You can donate to causes you believe in using Do Good Points. For every donation you make, you earn points towards rewards. If your purpose is just to donate, you're better off donating directly to the charity, so they don't incur any costs. But if you need an incentive to give, this is an excellent way to go.

Chapter 132 Become a Parts Model

Unlike traditional modeling agencies, a parts agency wants only pictures of body parts such as hands, feet, lips, eyes, skin, legs, butt, etc. Agencies such as Closeup Models Agency or Star Touch Agency use the pictures for company marketing programs.

Chapter 133 Get Paid to Go on a Date

Get reimbursed for the time and money it takes to prepare for a first date. The dating site WhatsYourPrice.com lets suitors pay women to go on dates with them. Quickly meet exciting and new people to go on fun dates. Online dating where you can buy & sell first dates. The easy way to meet wealthy and attractive people who otherwise may be out of your league.

Chapter 134 Become a Hostess

Hostesses are the modern counterpart of geishas, providing entertainment and company to men after work. They typically work in bars and get paid tips for dancing with men, sitting and talking, and often receive a percentage of the patrons' food and drinks. The pay can be into the thousands per night if the hostess can develop good listening skills and empathize with the patron's problems. They are often taking on the role of a therapist.

Chapter 135 Seamstress

Most people learn how to alter clothes as a hobby, but some go to college to learn fashion design. Because of the phasing out of home economics in high schools, there is a scarcity of seamstresses. The opportunities are boundless. You can offer your services at just about any clothing store.

Chapter 136 Make Money Saving Energy

The #OhmHour is a time when demand on the energy grid is so high that utility companies would rather pay their customers to reduce their common usage than firing up a dirtier "peaker" plant that may do more damage to the environment.

The utility will let OhmConnect know when to expect a time of intense demand, and they, in turn, will notify members about it via email or SMS. OhmConnect members will reduce their energy usage by turning off lights and appliances. If you've used less energy than you were forecasted, you get rewarded with cash payments or an entry into a bi-weekly prize draw. On average OhmConnect members get paid $100-$300 a year via PayPal. You can save even more if you live in a larger home. The service is free, and all you have to do is link your utility bill to OhmConnect.

Chapter 137 Earn with the Achievement App

The Achievement App connects with your phone health apps and helps gather data for medical research. You earn points for activities such as walking, meditating, logging meals, answering questions about yourself, and the healthy decisions you make. You trade those points in for cash. If you're looking to get fitter, this is an excellent option to help coordinate your health apps.

Chapter 138 Wrap Your Car in Ads

You may have seen cars or buses driving around town that have advertising wrapped on the outside. You can participate in this, by allowing Carvertise or Wrapify to wrap their advertisements on your vehicle. They will pay you for either a partial wrap or a full wrap of your car. The advertising agreements are usually for 1-2 months, then they'll over you a new wrap to continue generating income.

Chapter 139 Human Directional

A human directional is also known as a sign spinner. A spinner wears a costume and spins a sign while standing outside a business attracting attention to the company or product they're advertising. The work is outdoors, physical, and is in most demand when people are out and about.

Chapter 140 Earn Five Dollars per Month with SurveySavvy

Download the SurveySavvy app, and you'll get five dollars per device; tablet, phone, and computer. This app collects data on your device usage and reports it to the market research company. They compile this information and sell it to clients who are looking to market to people in your age group and demographic.

Chapter 141 Sell Your Smartphone Photos

You can upload and sell your photos on websites like Zenfolio or Foap. You sell the license to use your photos. When someone buys your picture for $10, you get half. If the same photo sells ten times, then you get $50 and so on. As long as your photos are listed, you can keep reselling the same images. We have wildflower blooms in southern California, and this year was one of the best. I took tons of pictures, just because I like taking pictures of them anyway, posted them to try this app out and people have been buying them. It's an excellent way to make something productive that sometimes is not very productive.

Chapter 142 Lend Your Clothes

I had a tenant who had a master's degree in marketing from the University of Southern California (USC), and she became a professional shopper. Her job was to shop for items at department stores for both movie studios and individuals to create looks and styles according to what the person needed to project. She was an expert in clothes. If you have particular expertise such as hers, look for creative ways to leverage your knowledge. Style Lend and LendMyTrend allow for peer-to-peer clothes lending to generate income.

Chapter 143 Crowdfund Your Business Idea

If you have an invention or a business idea that has promise, you can crowdfund it with Kickstarter, GoFundMe, or Indiegogo. These sites will allow you to raise capital so you can grow your business. Lots of people have ideas, but most people don't try to make something out of their concept. If money is one of your primary reasons for not taking action, crowdfunding is an excellent way to pursue your idea. There are three things I like about crowdfunding: First, we all think we have good ideas, but is it a good enough idea that others would want to buy or invest in that idea? Second, even if you don't need the money, posting an idea on a crowdfunding site is an excellent way to get some honest feedback on how good your idea might be. People will ask questions about things you may not have considered and comment on the weaknesses of your business idea. Both of these give you time to adjust your plan and improve it, before making a more significant investment. Third, there is the financing component, which can provide you with something to launch your idea with, to attract more investment.

If you're concerned about someone else capitalizing on your idea, you can patent or copyright your concept before you start the crowdfunding process.

Chapter 144 Product Licensing

Product licensing is an easy way for an inventor to turn their idea into a product. Licensing your product to someone else is faster, requires less investment from you, and can be more profitable than starting a new company to sell an invention.

How to license a product:

Come up with a new concept.

Patent your intellectual property through the United States Patent and Trademark Office (USPTO).

License a company to make and distribute your product.

Collect royalties.

Product licensing gives you a good balance of risk and reward. It enables large companies to reduce their internal research and development costs by partnering with outside entrepreneurs. Inventors rent or license their ideas to a company, which manufactures and distributes the product quickly and easily.

You may not want to license your product if you succeed on a crowdsourcing platform in some cases. Or because you found a big company like Sears or Nike that wants to buy and own your intellectual property rights. If you can make a good deal, it could sometimes be in your best interest to sell instead of a license.

Chapter 145 Rent Baby Gear

Another niche that can be explored; if you have a baby who's outgrown their baby gear, you can rent them out and make some additional revenue. GoBaby is a peer-to-peer lending site that allows you to rent out baby gear wherever you go.

Chapter 146 Get Free Beer

You can become a beer taster for Secret Hopper, sampling beer at bars and tasting rooms, and getting paid for it. Similar to a secret shopper, breweries pay Secret Hopper to send beer drinkers in to evaluate their product. The beer taster gives feedback to Secret Hopper more on customer service, atmosphere and location than the beer. Secret Hopper then shares this information with the brewery to help them improve and grow their business.

Chapter 147 Make Money Entering Online Contests and Giveaways

Online-Sweepstakes.com and Publishers Clearing House have new sweepstakes every day. They send you special offers, marketing materials, and games to participate in, and you're entered for chances to win prizes. The prizes range from samples of new products to thousands of dollars. They also send you a lot of spam so use an alternative email address.

Chapter 148 Avoid Multi-Level Marketing (MLM)

Multi-level marketing, also known as MLM programs, such as Amway or Herbalife, is not designed to help you, but to benefit owners and shareholders. There are hundreds of MLM companies. The U.S. Federal Trade Commission (FTC) states: "Stay clear of multilevel marketing plans that pay commissions for recruiting new distributors. They are illegal pyramid schemes." For the amount of effort, you have to invest in these programs, you're better off working for yourself. I've met people who have done really well in these programs, but it's usually at a cost to the poorest and less educated amongst us.

Chapter 149 Become a Small Business Consultant

Depending on what your expertise is in the business arena, you can leverage your knowledge to become a consultant for other businesses. Teaching businesses about social media marketing, recommending strategies to grow the business, suggestions for product development, product placement, store design, merchandising, workflow management, accounting strategies. The possibilities are virtually endless and depend more on your special skills or the special skills you're willing to develop so you can offer them to businesses.

Chapter 150 Collect Recyclables

You can collect cans, e-waste, bottles, ink cartridges, or metals to be traded in for cash. I used to collect recyclables with my friend Alexis, and we used to make enough money to go out to dinner and buy baseball cards.

Chapter 151 Sell Your Hair

Websites such as BuyandSellHair.com, OnlineHairAffair.com, and HairSellon are marketplaces for people to sell their hair to others. Human hair is in high demand for people who want real human hair extensions or have problems growing their own hair.

HairSellon has a "hair price calculator" that tells you exactly how much your hair is worth.

Chapter 152 Snag a job

Snag has temporary, part-time, and full-time gigs close to you. They are similar to a job website, except they're more proactive actually matching you with specific jobs. Snag offers jobs in all industries that you can start on short notice. They're not an agency, but they offer more than the usual job search website.

Chapter 153 Party Rentals

A rental business can be one of the most flexible, expanding, and scalable enterprises to start. Begin with one segment of the market that fits your budget and invest in marketing the service, and as your business grows, you can add more of the item you rent or add different offerings based on what customer requests. Start small with jumpers, tables, chairs, food machines, or decor. Then upgrade to higher-end offerings that bring in more profits, such as linens, party boats, party buses, limousines, beverage systems, watercraft, electric scooters, party characters, or outdoor activity/sporting equipment.

Chapter 154 Become a Bartender

Becoming a bartender is very fast to learn, and the opportunities are plentiful for those who are flexible. Bartenders can work nights, weekends, days, private parties, big parties, events, just about anywhere there is anything to celebrate or to do. Therefore, it's easy for you to find a niche to fill and earn some additional income.

No formal education is required to become a bartender and most people learn the trade on the job. First, you start as a barback and work your way up to a bartender. However, some bartenders learn their skills by attending bartending classes at a vocational or technical school.

Chapter 155 Become a Brand Ambassador

A brand ambassador works for a company or organization raising brand awareness and increasing sales. They work promoting products or services in-store or online. The majority of brand ambassadors host events, parties, and post on social media marketing the products of the brand.

How to become a Brand Ambassador:

1. Create an engaging social media profile.

Create your image and brand. Differentiate yourself from others. Make it enjoyable so that people will want to follow you, and you can build your social media follower count. The more people you have following you, the more likely a brand would want to invest in you. Make a positive and happy impression on the people following you. Make sure you're picking popular hashtags and keywords for your social media posts so that you can be easily found in searches.

2. Post awesome content.

Make sure you're posting engaging content, so you're able to attract more followers and brands. Stick to creating content that is geared towards the niche and group of followers you're trying to reach. You'll need to keep creating exciting content to keep people coming back for more.

3. Be consistent on social media.

Brands will ignore the number of followers you have if you're not engaged with your audience. They want to see you having conversations with your followers and that they see you as someone they can trust and value your opinion. Brands want to see a high engagement rate with your followers.

5. Be familiar with your audience.

Remember, having lots of followers is not enough. Brands want to see that you have a connection with your audience before they hire you as a brand ambassador. Grow an audience that is interested in the types of brands you want to represent. Create content that will attract the kinds of an audience that the brand will be interested in.

4. Create a personalized hashtag.

Make a hashtag that represents you as a brand. This will keep your posts organized and demonstrate to brands that you know what you're doing.

5. Sign up with a brand network.

After you have an established profile, followers, and engagement. The easiest way to get started is to sign up with a brand network site that facilitates the whole process for you. Set up an influencer profile on websites like Socialstars, Socialix, or Collectively. Upload your information, status, and they will guide you the rest of the way.

6. Be passionate.

There is a lot of competition, so you have to be consistent and stand out. To become a brand ambassador, you have to be focused, consistent, and invest time.

7. Start with small businesses and start-ups.

Small businesses and start-ups look for "micro-influencers" instead of well-established influencers because they're less expensive to contract with. If you start with small companies, it'll be easier to get started, and you can build your brand along the way. This approach usually cuts the amount of time you need to get bigger deals in half.

8. Focus on your interests and hobbies.

If you're not sure what market to focus on, start with niches that you have expertise in or have an interest in. People will be able to tell if you have knowledge or passion about what you're doing, so start with areas you're familiar with.

9. Start with brands that you would recommend and appreciate.

Promote brands that you enjoy and would be able to integrate into your lifestyle. If you're not sincere about a product, your fans will be able to tell that you're not a real fan of it. You should feel comfortable embracing and promoting a company that you would support even if you didn't work for them. This will make you appear more genuine, and people will trust you more.

11. Make a webpage that promotes your interest in possible brands to learn more about you.

Explain what you can offer to the brand and with what types of companies you're seeking partnership.

12. Be professional.

People are going to make negative comments and try to drag you into the dirt. Avoid the drama, be humble, stay polite, and always show a positive face through your account. Remove anything from the past that is not professional or may show you in a negative light.

13. Learn how the marketing game works.

Learn the basics of online marketing, brands want people who know what they're doing. Learn strategies on YouTube and through online courses on how to improve your social media presence. Implement the plans you're learning along the way, you'll get feedback immediately.

14. Advertise yourself.

Brands want people who have a strong network around them. Wherever you go, let people know about you.

15. Don't buy followers.

Brands have multiple ways to know if you bought followers, so don't, it will blacklist you. They'll check your engagement, and you'll lose opportunities.

You can use this outline to learn how to make money on YouTube or Instagram, or to get paid to travel as a brand ambassador.

Chapter 156 Become a Notary

A notary signing agent is a public servant. Each state appoints the notary to act as an impartial official to witness the signing of official documents and administer oaths. The course of study is very fast and typically only costs around $100. There are lots of job opportunities; you can be self-employed, and the work is reliable. I've paid up to $150 for a mobile notary to meet with me and notarize loan documents. And it took less than 20 minutes.

Chapter 157 Be a Coach for a Specific Sport

If you have experience in a sport or are willing to learn the sport, you can get paid to coach. I played college basketball and baseball as a kid. This helped me become a coach in both sports for teenagers. When parents wanted private lessons, they would hire me to teach their kids fundamentals such as the fundamentals of shooting mechanics.

Chapter 158 Newspaper Delivery

It's a great way to get exercise and see different neighborhoods, although nowadays, people tend to deliver newspapers by car. A newspaper delivery person is usually compensated per unit delivered along their route. Try your local newspaper and JobGolem for newspaper delivery jobs locally.

Chapter 159 Answer Professional Questions

If you have some high-level training or area of specific training, you can help others resolve problems and answer questions to help them solve them on their own. Websites, like JustAnswer, pay you to answer professional questions for folks needing questions answered. Just make sure you're actually an expert in the field you're fielding questions.

Chapter 160 Be a Movie Extra

To work as a movie extra is an amazing experience which allows you to see how one of the most famous industries on the planet operates. It also gives you an opportunity to participate, to learn about its inner workings, and to take on more roles in the future. Maybe even becoming a movie star yourself. If you live in Los Angeles, New York, or some other big city in the world, you can sign up for movie-extra work through Central Casting, Backstage, or other sites. You usually get free lunch and get paid for a day whether you stay the whole day or not and participate as needed.

Chapter 161 Become a Tour Guide

You can start out in your own city, and then become a tour guide taking people all over the planet. If you live in a vacation destination, you can offer your services as a tour guide. You can provide your services for a fee or for free, asking for tips at the end of the tour.

My friend Tony works for a Chinese travel agency here in Los Angeles. He had a group of fifty people coming from Indonesia who specifically requested an English-speaking American tour guide. So, he asked me if I could help him out for a few days. It was an amazing experience for all of us. The people were very curious, and they asked me dozens of questions throughout the day about every aspect of my life. Whenever we went to a new tourist site, each of them would line up and wanted to have their picture taken with me one by one. Everyone was very kind and appreciative. I got paid to go to Sea World, Tijuana, San Diego Zoo, and San Diego Wild Animal Park.

Chapter 162 Use Some of Your Liabilities to Generate Income

My cousin Brian Jones was trying to figure out how to make extra income because his liabilities were greater than his income. His answer was parked in his driveway, his motorhome. It went from costing him $600 in payments and insurance a month to generating $3000 a month renting his RV when he wasn't using it. Websites such as Outdoorsy or RVshare allow you to list your RV and start earning revenue when you're not using it. Both sites insure your vehicle for one million dollars and provide roadside assistance.

Chapter 163 Freelance Design Work

Offer your unique skills on Fiverr, Working Not Working, DesignCrowd, Dribbble, Smashing Magazine, Behance, Coroflot, Envato Studio, Design Crowd, ArtWanted.com, AngelList, and 99 Designs. These sites offer a variety of freelance work for designers of all types. They also give you the flexibility to work remotely and from anywhere in the world. The better the quality of work you produce, the better your reputation, and the more income you'll make over the long run. If you have a special talent for making crafts, you can make items and sell them on Etsy or CafePress. Some of the other websites you can check out for freelance work are SolidGigs, Servicescape, CloudPeeps, Freelancer.com, College Recruiter, or Craigslist that will allow you to leverage your unique skills to help others. You can list skills such as web design, card reading, psychics, translating if you're bilingual, copywriting, music lessons, virtual assistant, bartender, notary, graphic design for logos, DJ, t-shirts, banners etc, interior design consulting, wedding planner, transcribing audio to written words, or electronics repair.

Chapter 164 Recruiter

Due to a shortage of skilled staff, companies are willing to pay someone to help them find workers to fill positions. You can be a freelance recruiter and the work can be done remotely. The recruiter evaluates people's qualifications, experience, and negotiate salaries. You post ads, send letters, and scour the internet job boards looking for people qualified to fill positions. As you find them, you are paid a fee for filling the positions. Indeed and FlexJobs are among many other websites that have listings for recruiters working for companies all over the world.

Chapter 165 Work for Customer Support

These jobs are very flexible in hours and you can typically work from anywhere. You help answer questions and hear complaints from customers as a representative for a company. We Work Remotely, Support Driven, and Virtual Vocations are all websites you can browse to find part time, full time, or flexible job hours doing customer support. If you prefer sales to customers, try Red Hat, Salesforce, or SkipTheDrive.

My cousin Veronica works as a customer service representative for a cruise line. When folks have issues or questions about their cruise, they call the 800 number, and the call is routed to her headpiece. She answers calls and questions from customers during her work hours from home. This allows her to be available to her kids when they need her and to complete her housework.

Chapter 166 Become a Freelance Photographer, Film, or Video Editor

Another extremely flexible gig that allows you to hang out at parties and other events is photography or videography. Most of the freelance sites mentioned offer photographer work, but here are some extra specialized sites; JournalismJobs.com, Airbnb, CruiseShipJobs.com, Creative Jobs Central, Photography Jobs Finder, and Photography-Jobs.net. Video editing is also in high demand with indie films and YouTubers becoming popular. The best sites to find video editing work is Mandy, Stage 32, Assemble, and ProductionHUB.

Chapter 167 Become a Virtual Assistant

Virtual assistants are like secretaries or executive assistants; they help you complete office work. Some of the best sites to work as a virtual assistant and to find one to help you manage your workload once you become successful are Upwork, BELAY, Time etc, Worldwide101, Clickworker, VAnetworking, Assistant Match, Fancy Hands, and Zirtual. Virtual assistance gives you a great deal of flexibility. They allow you to scale up your business to handle extra work when needed; and if things slow down, it allows you to easily scale down till you need the extra work again.

Chapter 168 Work as an Online Juror

By joining the website eJury.com, you can get paid to participate in mock jury trials online to help attorneys practice their court skills. This experience would also help you if you're trying to decide whether or not to become an attorney. Seeing what a trial is like could be a good preview and would be a good experience in case you ever have to go to court.

Chapter 169 Rent Out Your Stuff

You can make money renting your items, such as ski equipment, bikes, video equipment, music equipment, or anything else people may want, allowing you to generate revenue with things you have at home. There are several websites such as PeerRenters, BorrowLenses.com, or Skipti to help you find people to rent your stuff. The best part is that your belongings are insured. If you find items that are in high demand, you can buy more of those items for the purpose of renting them out. My neighbor is a cameraman and has high-end video equipment that he is renting on these sites. He's able to make several thousand a month on an ongoing basis.

Chapter 170 Food Trucks

Suppose you are interested in opening your restaurant but prefer lower start-up costs. A food truck is a good alternative, with the most considerable expense being the truck itself, ranging from $15,000 to $100,000. The Food Trucks industry in the US is $1.3bn in 2021 and grows around 3.9% per year.

A food truck allows you to fill a niche market, moving to where the clients are to cook, prepare, serve, and sell food. The on-board kitchen will enable you to prepare food from scratch or heat food prepared in a brick-and-mortar commercial kitchen.

Chapter 171 Street Vendor

Street vendors can sell personal items such as toys, t-shirts, souvenirs, or food items such as tacos, fruit, corn, popcorn, cotton candy, candy apples, hot dogs, or most other snack foods. Once you get local permits and licenses, you want to look for high-traffic areas, such as business districts or college towns, to set up shop. Some of the benefits include low start-up costs, low overhead, and the ability to move the stand if the original location turns out to be less than ideal or the competition from other vendors is too fierce.

Chapter 172 Buy and Sell Vintage Clothes

During the coronavirus quarantine, my young hip neighbors introduced me to the world of online vintage clothing sales. While most people's jobs were on hold, their online business was booming.

Millennials try to stay away from "fast fashion" mass-produced clothing that is not environmentally friendly and has no soul. Instead, they seek clothing that teaches you the history of fashion, recycled, and allows you to walk into a bar wearing clothes that most likely no one else has.

Start by digging for clothes at second-hand shops,

used clothing by the pound stores, the Rose Bowl (the world's largest flea market), The Goodwill, The Salvation Army, or "rag shops." Fashion savvy people can pick up old concert and rock band t-shirts that can fetch hundreds and even thousands online. Old denim jeans can go for one hundred dollars, with only a five-dollar investment. By investing a few hours, a month searching for clothes, taking pictures, and posting online, you can add an extra thousand dollars a month. Good places to look for and sell clothing are Poshmark, Depop, Mercari, Etsy, or eBay. Although Poshmark is one of the most popular to buy and sell new or used clothing, shoes, and accessories, it allows you to set up a virtual closet for your customers to browse through.

Chapter 173 Junk Removal

A few years ago, I had a tenant moving out, and I needed the items they had left behind removed so that I could clean the space and offer it for rent again. I checked on craigslist, and I saw an ad that read, "Are you moving and need trash removed? Call me. I'll do it for Free". So, I contacted the "picker," and he kindly came over and helped me empty the space. As he worked removing the items, I asked him about his business model, and he was gracious enough to take me to his yard and show me exactly what he did. He explained to me that he was a picker, and his job was to travel around in his truck, removing junk for people, hauling the items back home, and separating them into categories for resale. Metals for recycling, high-value items for eBay, OfferUp, and craigslist, donations, and other things he would resell to people who had stalls at swap meets. The yard was also a showroom for customers to shop from; it reminded me of the television show "Sanford and Sons." I ended up buying some articles I needed for my projects, and he shared with me that he averaged around ten thousand dollars a month being a junk remover and picker. His wife worked as his assistant packing and shipping items that were sold online and showed me a stack of two thousand dollars' worth of packages ready to ship. Some people make additional income charging for the service of junk removal, and they profit off from selling the items they collect as well.

Chapter 174 Medical Billing

In medical or dental offices, there is a lot of variation in workflows. As one day, the doctor may be in the office seeing patients, then not be back in the office for two-three days. Therefore, paperwork is typically completed on the days that the doctor is not in the office, and appointment days are solely for patient care. Coding and medical billing can be a time-consuming, repetitive process that most doctors outsource. Outsourcing medical billing allows physicians to increase productivity by enabling them to focus on seeing and treating patients.

Websites such as eAssist or AdvancedMD allow you to train online and work at home as a medical biller and coder, earning $20-$35 an hour. The more familiar you become with the codes, the faster you'll be able to bill and increase your income.

Conclusion

T his collection of ideas for generating additional income covers a variety of techniques for a broad spectrum of income levels, education, and experience so that everyone can have an opportunity to grow their revenue no matter where they are on the income ladder. These strategies will not make sense to everyone, but there are some that can be used by all. Try to start with the strategies that work for you and try leveraging up with the more unfamiliar ones as you build your wealth and diversify your income. Often people are searching for ways to increase their income; they should first analyze their current situation and figure out how to maximize their current potential with what they have access to. There are several ways to do so by saving on taxes, saving on fixed expenses, or by growing businesses and activities you are already involved in to make more money. The first step should be the easiest, utilize the knowledge, skills, and abilities (KSA) you already have to get started.

To develop new business ideas, look at what people are doing around you. You don't have to reinvent the wheel; redesign or repurpose ideas to create new businesses or concepts.

When you are considering or developing business ideas, ask yourself are you solving a problem that people have? Are you addressing a need in the marketplace? Ask yourself, is there an obvious way to make money from this idea? Is the time you're going to invest in this gig worth your effort? In other words, is the opportunity cost high enough for you to do it? If you are a barber and you can cut someone's hair for $20 an hour, you don't want to spend time messing with apps for $10 an hour. The $10 job is useful if you don't have anyone's hair to cut; then it would make sense. Otherwise, stick to the work that pays the most, unless your goal is to acquire a new skill so you can follow another plan. Ask yourself is this new business going to keep bringing money in or is it a one-time gig. These questions should all be answered with your financial plan so that you have a game plan for achieving your goals.

Don't be afraid to go out on your own; self-employed people are four times more likely to become millionaires than people who work for others. Eighty percent of millionaires in America are first-generation rich people. Rich people don't inherit their wealth as many people think, they go out and earn it themselves. The most common way to do so is by starting your own business.

If you have kids, start teaching them about money. Research shows that the more money you give your kids, the less wealth they accumulate. Therefore, giving money to children damages their ability to succeed in life. It also shows that wealthy people are more likely to have rich children because they teach their kids how to be rich.

In the end, money has a different meaning for each one of us; for some of us it is status, and even though you're living in a house of cards, it feels good to show others what you've accomplished and have to show for it. On the other hand, you can have freedom. For me money represents freedom. Freedom to live as you want and make decisions without having to worry about money and its restraints. Freedom to live the life you've always wanted to live and set your course. But money should never be the most important thing in your life. Health, family, happiness, and then money should be your priority.

You can render no greater service to God and humanity than making the most of yourself.

ABOUT THE AUTHOR

Dr. Ernesto Martinez suffered a near-fatal assault that changed the direction of his life. The experience helped him acquire a greater moral understanding and develop greater empathy for others.

Martinez is a Naturopathic Doctor, Occupational Therapist, and Investor. He also enjoys writing, publishing, traveling, blogging AttaBoyCowboy.com, and running his YouTube channel AttaBoyCowboy.

So be sure to check out his fun books, blog, and YouTube channel.

Martinez's work as a Naturopathic Doctor specializes in anti-aging medicine and complementary cancer therapies. He focuses on a whole-body treatment approach utilizing safe natural methods, while simultaneously restoring the body's natural ability to heal.

His work as an Occupational Therapist has allowed him to help people across the lifespan to do things they want and need to do to live their life to the fullest. His strong desire to mentor and help others has led him to teach, share, and help them live better lives.

As an Investor, Martinez has focused his training and business acumen on real estate. With a family history of real estate investing and extensive academic training, he has developed innovative strategies for building wealth from nothing.

In addition to his medical practice and three decades of investing experience, Martinez is making his impact on the writing and media field. Through his books, blog, and YouTube channel, he is reaching a broad spectrum of people and teaching them how to live healthier and wealthier lives.

Martinez has taught extension courses at the University of San Diego in topics ranging from nutrition and general health to leadership and business. He holds five associate degrees from Cerritos College, a bachelor's degree from the University of Southern California (USC), an MBA in economics and marketing, and a master's degree in healthcare management (MHCM) from California State University Los Angeles (CSULA), a doctoral degree from Clayton College, and over ten other degrees and advanced certifications in areas including lifestyle redesign and nutrition, alternative nutrition, assistive technology, sensory integration, neuro-developmental treatment, physical agent modalities, lymphedema treatment, and property management. He studied over fifteen years working his entire academic career and for several years attending two graduate schools on two separate campuses at the same time.

He is a huge fan of all sports, reading, and being on the road traveling!

As an entrepreneur, Ernesto is usually problem-solving business issues, writing, and learning to be a better person. He enjoys spending time with his family and friends.

By far one of his favorite activities is practicing his Random Acts of Kindness, where he tries to do three acts of kindness for strangers a day.

Bonus

Top Ten Ways to Decrease Your Environmental Impact During Travel per World Wildlife Fund (WWF)

1. Go on holiday during the off-peak period to prevent overstraining resources; you'll also avoid the crowds.

2. Find out about places before you visit. You may be visiting an environmentally sensitive area, in which case you must take extra care to stay on footpaths and follow signs.

3. Don't travel by air if you can avoid it, because air travel uses up large amounts of jet fuel that releases greenhouse gases.

4. Dispose of any rubbish responsibly; it can be hazardous to wildlife.

5. Use public transportation, cycle or walk instead of using a car.

6. Use facilities and trips run by local people whenever possible.

7. Don't be tempted to touch wildlife and disturb habitats whether on land, at the coast, or under water.

8. Be careful what you choose to bring home as a holiday souvenir. Many species from coral and conch shells to elephants and alligators are endangered because they are killed for curios or souvenirs.

9. Don't dump chemicals into the environment; it can be very dangerous for wildlife.

10. Boats and jet-skis create noise and chemical pollution that is very disturbing to wildlife; don't keep the engine running unnecessarily

Top Ten Ways to Decrease Your Environmental Impact after Travel per WWF

1. Completely turn off equipment like televisions and stereos when you're not using them.

2. Choose energy-efficient appliances and light bulbs.

3. Save water: some simple steps can go a long way in saving water, like turning off the tap when you are brushing your teeth or shaving. Try to collect the water used to wash vegetables and salad to water your houseplants.

4. Lower your shades or close your curtains on hot days, to keep the house fresh and reduce the use of electric fans or air-conditioning.

5. Let clothes dry naturally.

6. Keep lids on pans when cooking to conserve energy.

7. Use rechargeable batteries.

8. Call your local government to see if they have a disposal location for used batteries, glass, plastics, paper, or other wastes.

9. Don't use "throwaway" products like paper plates and napkins or plastic knives, forks, and cups.

10. Send electronic greetings over email instead of paper cards.

Top Ten Ways to Decrease Your Environmental Impact in the Garden per WWF

1. Collect rainwater to water your garden.

2. Water the garden early in the morning or late in the evening. Water loss is reduced due to evaporation. Don't over-water the garden. Water only until the soil

becomes moist, not soggy.

3. Explore water-efficient irrigation systems. Sprinkler irrigation and drip irrigation can be adapted to garden situations.

4. Make your garden lively, plant trees, and shrubs that will attract birds. You can also put up bird nest boxes with food.

5. Put waste to work in your garden, sweep the fallen leaves and flowers into flowerbeds, or under shrubs. Increasing soil fertility and also reduce the need for frequent watering.

6. If you have little space in your garden, you could make a compost pit to turn organic waste from the kitchen and garden to soil-enriching manure.

7. Plant local species of trees, flowers, and vegetables.

8. Don't use chemicals in the garden, as they will eventually end up in the water systems and can upset the delicate balance of life cycles.

9. Organic and environmentally friendly fertilizers and pesticides are available - organic gardening reduces pollution and is better for wildlife.

10. Buy fruit and vegetables that are in season to help reduce enormous transport costs resulting from importing products and, where possible, choose locally produced food.

Top Ten Ways to Reduce, Reuse, and Recycle per WWF

1. Use email to stay in touch, including cards, rather than faxing or writing.

2. Share magazines with friends and pass them on to

the doctor, dentist, or local hospital for their waiting rooms.

3. Use recyclable paper to make invitation cards, envelopes, letter pads, etc. if you can.

4. Use washable nappies instead of disposables, if you can.

5. Recycle as much as you can.

6. Give unwanted clothes, toys, and books to charities and orphanages.

7. Store food and other products in containers rather than foil and plastic wrap.

8. When buying fish, look out for a variety of non-endangered species, and buy local fish if possible.

9. Bring your bags to the grocery and refuse plastic bags that create so much waste.

10. Look for products that have less packaging.

Top Ten Ways to Reduce Your Environmental Impact at Work per WWF

1. Always use both sides of a sheet of paper.

2. Use printers that can print on both sides of the paper; try to look into this option when replacing old printers.

3. Use the back of a draft or unwanted printout instead of notebooks. Even with a double-sided printer, there is likely to be plenty of spare paper to use!

4. Always ask for and buy recycled paper if you can, for your business stationery, and to use it in your printers.

5. Switch off computer monitors, printers, and other

equipment at the end of each day. Always turn off your office light and computer monitor when you go out for lunch or to a meeting.

6. Look for power-saving alternatives like LED light bulbs, motion-sensing to control the lighting, LED computer monitors, etc. Prioritize buying or replacing equipment and appliances with their higher Energy Rating alternatives.

7. Contact your energy provider and what they offer in the way of green energy alternatives. You could install solar panels to reduce reliance on energy providers if they're slow on the green energy uptake.

8. Carpool. Ask your workmates that live nearby if they'd be happy to share rides with you.

9. Be smarter with your company vehicles. When reviewing your fleet, spend some time researching more efficient cars.

10. Clean and maintain equipment regularly to extend their useful life and avoid having to replace them. Just like getting your vehicle serviced regularly, your floors, kitchens, equipment, and bathrooms all need regular attention to protect their form and function.

Made in the USA
Las Vegas, NV
06 July 2021

26053805R00069